TORAH
TEACHERS
and
YOU

by
SOL SCHARFSTEIN

Illustrated by
Arthur Freedman

KTAV PUBLISHING HOUSE, INC • HOBOKEN • NEW JERSEY

Contents

Introduction:

Look at this map of the ancient Middle East. Notice that at one end of the crescent lies the wealthy land of Babylonia. At the other edge you see the ancient and Powerful land of Egypt. Between these two great nations lies an ocean of hot dry sand—the Arabian desert.

Between these two powerful nations lies a bridge of land sandwiched in by the sea to the west and the desert to the east. That land is Palestine. Long ago, caravans of trade peacefully made their way between Babylonia and Egypt. In times of war, the caravans were replaced by marching soldiers and horse-drawn chariots.

You can see why each of the powerful nations wanted to own the land called Palestine. Whoever controlled Palestine—the land bridge—could stop the other country from invading. Whoever controlled the land bridge could tax the caravans carrying their rich loads of goods from one country to another.

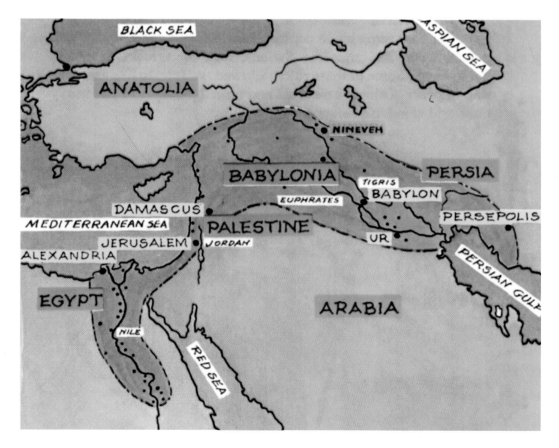

After the fall of Jerusalem in 586 B.C.E., other nations became powerful and were able to control Palestine: first the Babylonians, then the Persians, then the Syrians, then the Greeks, and then the Romans. Some of these rulers allowed the Jews to live and worship in peace. Other were cruel and forced the Jews to pay heavy taxes and worship strange gods.

SYRIAN

BABYLONIAN   PERSIAN

In time of trouble the rabbis, teachers, and leaders of Israel tried to keep the Jewish way of life alive. They taught the people to follow the laws of the Torah, to love God, and to live in a fair and honest way.

Our book is about some of the great rabbis and teachers who lived during these troubled times. You will learn how these heroes helped keep our people and our religion alive to this very day. The great civilizations of Babylonia, Persia, Greece, and Rome have all disappeared but the Jews and Israel live on.

Our book will also show how the Jews later had to leave Palestine and how they moved to France, Germany, Spain, and other countries of Europe as well as Asia and Africa. You will see how great leaders and rabbis helped keep the Jewish ways alive in times of trouble.

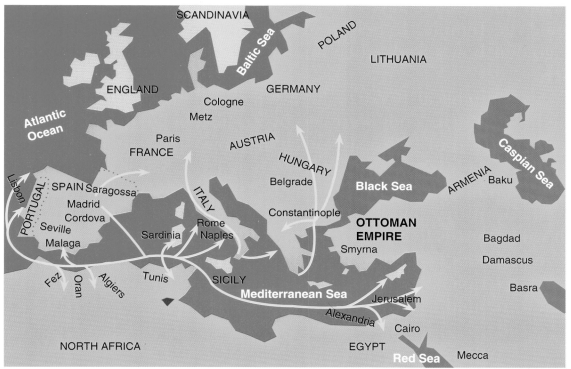

The expulsion from Spain in 1492. The map shows how the first exiles went to Portugal and southern Italy; persecution followed and many fled eastward to coutries of the Ottoman Empire.

World History: 6th century B.C.E.

IN 539 B.C.E., the Persians, led by Cyrus, defeated the Babylonian army. Cyrus was an enlightened conqueror and granted religious freedom to all the peoples in his huge empire, which extended from India to Egypt.

The exiled Jews of Babylon gained new hope from Cyrus's wise and tolerant policies. He gave them permission to return to Jerusalem and rebuild the Temple. To help restore the Temple's beauty, he gave them the golden bowls and other holy items which Nebuchadnezzar had stolen.

From the biblical Book of Ezra we learn that 42,000 Jews eagerly joined the return. They were led by Zerubbabel, the grandson of one of the last kings of Judea, Jehoiachim. Now they would once again be able to live a Jewish life in their own holy land. Sadly, they found their once-beautiful land in ruins. Fields and vineyards were overgrown with weeds. Towns that had once been busy and prosperous were deserted, with wild animals living in the ruined houses.

The pioneers did not waste time worrying about the present situation. They quickly cleared the fields, replanted the vineyards, and began to rebuild their homes.

In 586 B.C.E., when Babylon conquered Judea and destroyed the Temple, a number of Jews had been allowed to remain in the land. North of Judea, in what had been the Kingdom of Israel until the Assyrian conquest in the 8th  century B.C.E., lived many descendants of the tribes of Ephraim and Manasseh. Over the years they had intermarried with the pagan peoples brought in by the Assyrians after they deported the Ten Lost Tribes. Their religion was a mixture of idol worship and Judaism.

The people who lived in this area called themselves Samaritans because the city of Samaria, once the capital of Israel, was their main city. Considering themselves Israelites, they wanted to be a part of the restored nation. When the exiles returned, they offered to help rebuild the Temple.

The Jews from Babylon were determined to found a commonwealth based on the Torah. Since the Samaritans were really pagans with an Israelite veneer, they refused their offer.

The Samaritans now became their bitter enemies. They attacked the Judean settlements and burned their crops. They sent false reports to Cyrus alleging that the Jews were planning a revolt against him. The king believed them and called a halt to the rebuilding of the Temple.

The Samaritans were not the returning exiles' only enemy. Edomite and Moabite raiders attacked their farms, kidnapped the inhabitants, and stole the harvest.

For the Zionists of the First Return, the future was dark. Over the next fifty years, the dwindling numbers of colonists suffered enemy attacks, poor harvests, and heavy Persian taxes. The tiny state of Judea was in deep trouble.

Ezra and Nehemiah: 5th century B.C.E.

AMONG THE EXILES in Babylonia who were distressed by the news from Judea was Ezra, a learned man of priestly descent. Ezra was a dedicated teacher and had many students to whom he taught the Torah. Because he was highly skilled in the art of writing Torah scrolls, he is often referred to as Ezra the Scribe (*Ezra HaSofer*).

When Ezra asked King Artaxerxes I of Persia for permission to go to Jerusalem with his disciples, his request was granted. The king and the Jewish community of Babylonia generously gave Ezra many gifts for the Temple and also the supplies he needed for the long journey. Artaxerxes even sent along soldiers to protect the returnees.

The Second Return consisted of about 1,500 settlers eager to rebuild their homeland. They arrived in Jerusalem in the summer of 458 B.C.E. and were warmly welcomed by the tiny Jewish community.

Ezra began his task without delay. He was saddened and disturbed to find that the people lacked any knowledge of the Torah.

Patiently Ezra and his disciples encouraged them to resume the great struggle to regain their homeland and rebuild the Temple.

The next major task was to fortify Jerusalem against the hostile bands of raiders by rebuilding its walls.

Help came in 445 B.C.E. when Nehemiah, a Babylonian Jew, was appointed governor of Judea. Nehemiah had been the trusted cupbearer of King Artaxerxes I in Shushan (Susa), the Persian capital. A dedicated Zionist, he immediately set out for Judea, armed with royal credentials and authority.

The two great leaders of the returnees, Ezra and Nehemiah, combined their efforts to restore the commonwealth of Judea. Ezra was Judea's spiritual guide; Nehemiah, its political leader. His enthusiasm energized the people to rebuild the walls of Jerusalem.

The walls and fortifications were completed in just 52 days. Because of the constant threat of Samaritan attacks, the workers "did the work with one hand and held a weapon with the other." The people of Judea defended the walls fiercely, and the raiders soon began to think twice before they attacked.

Nehemiah and Ezra laid the foundations of the new Jewish commonwealth. The Torah was its constitution. Ezra and his students traveled throughout the land, teaching the people to live by its laws.

On the day before Sukkot in the year 444 B.C.E., thousands of Judeans made their way to Jerusalem. They built their sukkot in the ancient city of David, then assembled to hear from their two great leaders. Nehemiah and the priests and Levites of the Second Temple stood before the assembled Judeans, while Ezra read aloud from the Torah. The people, listening attentively, raised their hands and shouted "Amen, Amen." They promised to obey the laws of the Torah.

The work of Ezra and Nehemiah was followed by an era of peace for Judea. Towns and villages were rebuilt, land was tilled and cultivated. Many towns built their own marketplaces and houses of prayer.

Later on, these houses of prayer evolved into the synagogues which have become the centers of Jewish communal and religious life throughout the world.

MATCH THE COLUMNS

1. Persian	First Temple
2. Book of	Sofer
3. Samaritans	King Cyrus
4. Nehemiah	Ezra
5. Solomon's	Governor of Judea
6. Ezra	Ephraim and Manasseh

FILL IN THE BLANKS

1. Nehemiah and Ezra laid the foundation of the new _____ commonwealth.

2. The houses of prayer became the _____ of today.

3. _____ was an enlightened ruler and gave religious freedom to all.

4. Nehemiah was cupbearer in the court of King _____.

5. _____ was a learned Jew of priestly descent.

6. Ezra was the _____ guide, and _____ was the political leader.

King Cyrus, Ezra, Nehemiah, Artaxerxes, spiritual, synagogues, Jewish

ANSWER THE QUESTIONS

1. Why did the Jews want to return to Jerusalem?
2. Why did the Samaritans want to be part of the new nation?
3. Why did the Jews refuse the help of the Samaritans?
4. Can you think of a reason why Ezra was concerned about the lack of Torah knowledge among the people?
5. How did Ezra decide to remedy the situation?
6. What was the foundation of the new commonwealth?
7. Why did Ezra and Nehemiah make a good team?

EZRA AND YOU

In 444 B.C.E., the Jews gathered around the rebuilt Second Temple. After the opening ceremonies Ezra mounted the platform and read from the Torah.

Now in mid-September all the people assembled at the plaza in front of the Water Gate and requested Ezra, their religious leader, to read to them the law of God which He had given to Moses.

So Ezra, the priest, brought out to them the scroll of Moses' laws. Everyone stood up as He opened the scroll. And all who were old enough to understand paid close attention.

As Ezra read from the scroll the Levites went among the people and explained the meaning of the passage that was being read. All the people began sobbing when they heard the commands of the law.

1. Why did the people ask Ezra to read the Torah to them?
2. Why was it necessary for the Levites to explain the meaning of the passages?
3. Why did the rabbis decide to emphasize the reading of the Torah?
4. Do you think it is a good idea to read a portion of the Torah each week?
5. In what language did Ezra read the Torah?

DID YOU KNOW?

Throughout the Near East and especially in Babylonia and Syria, Aramaic was the main language. After the return from the Babylonian exile, it also became the everyday spoken language of Judea. Since the Torah was written in Hebrew, many people could no longer understand it when it was read aloud at synagogue services.

Ezra solved the problem by providing a translator, who stood next to the Torah reader and translated the Hebrew into Aramaic for the congregants. Eventually, these oral translations were set down in writing. The Aramaic translation of the Torah is called the Targum. Note the similarity between the word *meturgeman* ("translator") and the name Targum.

The Hebrew Bible is called the Tanak. The Tanak is divided into three divisions, Torah (Five Books of Moses), Neviim (Prophets), and Ketuvim (Writings). The name Tanak comes from the first letters of each of the three divisions, *T* is for Torah, *N* is for Neviim, and *K* is for Ketuvim.

There are a total of twenty-four separate books in the Tanak. The Torah has five books, the Prophets eight books, and the Writings eleven books. The language of the Tanak is Hebrew except for portions of the books of Daniel and Ezra which are in Aramaic.

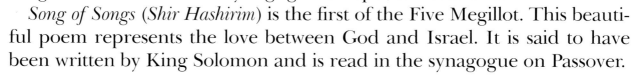

In addition to the books in the Tanak, the Jews of long ago wrote many other books, but over the centuries, most of them were lost. Some were preserved in a collection called the Apocrypha.

Included among the Ketuvim are five books called Scrolls (*Megillot*). The Five Megillot are read in the synagogue on special occasions.

Song of Songs (*Shir Hashirim*) is the first of the Five Megillot. This beautiful poem represents the love between God and Israel. It is said to have been written by King Solomon and is read in the synagogue on Passover.

The *Book of Ruth* is the second of the Five Megillot. It tells the story of Ruth, the Moabite great-grandmother of David. The Book of Ruth is read on Shavuot.

The Book of Lamentations (*Ekhah*) is the third of the Five Megillot. It contains songs of sorrow and is said to have been written by the prophet Jeremiah, mourning the destruction of Jerusalem and the Temple.

Lamentations is chanted on Tisha B'Av (ninth of the month of Av), the day commemorating that sad event.

The *Book of Ecclesiastes* (*Kohelet*) is the fourth of the Five Megillot. It is a book of wise sayings, one of the three biblical books said to have been written by King Solomon.

The Book of Esther (*Megillat Esther*) is the fifth of the Five Megillot. A peculiar feature of this scroll is that God's name is never mentioned. In spite of its lack of a religious aspect, the story of brave Queen Esther has always had a great impact on Jews. It is the earliest account of anti-Semitism in the bloodstained chronicle of Jewish history.

The biblical story of Esther took place in Shushan (Susa), the capital of Persia, in about 486–485 B.C.E. The king in the story is called Ahasuerus, probably a variation of the Persian name Xerxes. According to the Bible, his kingdom extended from Ethiopia to India and he ruled over 127 provinces.

Queen Esther 5th century B.C.E.

KING AHASUERUS commanded his wife, Queen Vashti, to dance for his drunken guests at a palace party. She did not wish to humiliate herself and refused to dance.

The angry king consulted his advisors, and they suggested that Vashti be immediately replaced and a new queen chosen.

Officials in all 127 provinces were instructed to choose the most beautiful girls, and send them to Susa for a beauty contest. The winner would become the new queen.

The contest was held and the winner was a Jewish girl named Esther.

Esther, the new queen, arranged an official position for her uncle Mordecai, and he was allowed to "sit in the King's Gate," where he observed the comings and goings of the palace officials.

King Ahasueras appointed a cruel and ambitious man called Haman as his chief minister. Everyone was ordered to show him respect by kneeling and bowing. As a proud Jew Mordecai refused to bow down to Haman. This angered Haman and he decided to punish Mordecai as well as all the Jews in Persia.

Haman went to Ahasuerus and said, "Their laws are different and they do not obey the king's rulings. Let them all be destroyed. I will pay ten thousand silver talents if you will issue such a decree."

Haman wanted to wipe out all the Jews in the Persian empire and seize their property and assets. Ahasuerus believed his chief advisor and agreed to the proposal.

Haman cast lots (*purim*) to choose the month and the day for the pogrom. The *purim* chose the fourteenth day of the month of Adar.

When Mordecai found out about the impending pogrom against the Jews, he urged Esther to save her people. At first, Esther refused to go to the king without official permission. But Mordecai persisted and said, "Do not imagine that you, of all Jews, will escape with your life. Who knows, perhaps you have attained this position for use in such a crisis." Esther violated a law that prohibited anyone from approaching the king without an official invitation. Esther bravely entered the throne room without permission and revealed that she was Jewish and that Haman's bloodthirsty plot would destroy her people.

The king loved Esther. He realized that Haman would use the Jewish pogrom to start a revolution and endanger his kingship.

Ahasuerus wisely decided to save his throne and eliminate Haman's competition. The king also decreed that Haman and his sons were to be hanged on the same gallows he had built for Mordecai. As a token of trust and thankfulness, he appointed Mordecai as one of his advisors and gave him Haman's signet ring.

Esther and Mordecai instituted the holiday of Purim to commemorate this great historical event. The name *purim* comes from the Hebrew word *pur,* meaning "lot."

Jews all over the world celebrate Purim by reading the story of brave Queen Esther in the Megillah. They exchange *shallach manot* gifts and sing and dance, hold masquerades, and eat three-cornered cakes called hamantashen.

Haman chose the day for the pogrom against the Jews by casting lots (*purim*). So today, Purim, the Feast of Lots, is celebrated on the fourteenth day of the Hebrew month of Adar.

The Scroll of Esther is read in the synagogue on Purim. Every time Haman's name is read, you stamp your feet, boo, and turn your groggers (noisemakers) trying to drown out Haman's evil name.

MATCH THE COLUMNS

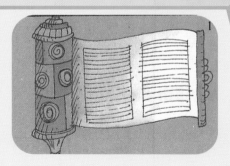

1. Tanak   Purim
2. Lamentations   Persian Queen
3. Ahasuerus   Hebrew Bible
4. 14th of Adar   Xerxes
5. Purim   Tisha B'Av
6. Esther   Feast of Lots

FILL IN THE BLANKS

1. The scroll of _____ is found in the section of the Tanak called _____

2. There are _____ books in the Tanak.

3. Ahasueras was king of _____

4. _____ refused to bow down to _____

5. The holiday of Purim is also called _____

6. Esther violated the law which prohibited anyone to approach the _____ without permission

Esther, Feast of Lots, Ketuvim, Haman, King, Mordecai, Persia, twenty-four,

ANSWER THE QUESTIONS

1. Why did the Persian king decide to get rid of Vashti?
2. What does the word *purim* mean?
3. Why did the king decide to get rid of Haman?
4. How do Jews celebrate the Feast of Lots?
5. Why do we celebrate Purim on the 14th day of Adar?
6. Who initiated the holiday of Purim?

ESTHER AND YOU

In ancient days, rulers were fearful of assassinations. The kings surrounded themselves with loyal soldiers and only allowed people into the throne room by special permission. Those who entered without an appointment or special credentials were immediately put to death. As a matter of history Xerxes, who may have been Ahasuerus, was assassinated by one of his "loyal" aides.

The Megillah tells us that Esther prepared herself by fasting for three days. Only then did she have the courage to enter the throne room unannounced. Throughout Jewish history, courageous women have performed acts of heroism.

In modern times, Hannah Senesh parachuted into German-held territory, but was captured and killed by the Nazis. Hundreds of Jewish girls fought and were murdered by the Germans in the Warsaw Ghetto uprising. Today, Israeli women fly combat planes, and some serve in front line fighting units. Theses are just a few of the "Esthers" who have fought for freedom and performed deeds of valor.

Esther took a stand that endangered her life. In real life, there comes a time when a brother, sister, relative, or friend needs someone to stick up for them and take a stand.

Sticking up takes courage, but it is the right thing to do. Esther could have lived a life of luxury in the palace. But fate gave her the opportunity to save the lives of tens of thousands of Jews, and without hesitation she took it. Her timing was right, and she acted, even though it might have meant her death.

Talk to your rabbi, to your parents, or teacher about ways you can stand up and help people and groups in need. Think about the opportunities around you and what you can do to take advantage of them.

You are an important person, and you have the power to do much good. Don't miss your chance!

World History: 1st century B.C.E.

IN 40 B.C.E., HEROD, whose family had converted to Judaism, was crowned king of Judea by the Roman Senate. He was a brilliant administrator but was very cruel to those he ruled.

While the people of Judea hated and feared Herod, the Romans valued him as an ally. During his reign Judea's prosperity increased.

Herod delighted in massive building projects. He founded two new cities in honor of his Roman friends: Tiberias, named for Tiberius, Rome's second emperor, and the coastal city of Caesarea, named for Augustus Caesar, its first emperor. He also built many fortresses, including Masada, near the Dead Sea, as well as arenas where gladiators fought to the death and helpless captives were pitted against wild animals.

Herod's most ambitious project was the reconstruction of the Temple. This was a huge task that took many years to complete. His workmen and architects renovated and completely rebuilt the Second Temple dating from the time of Ezra and Nehemiah. They began in 20 B.C.E. and did not finish until several years after Herod's death.

Herod's Temple was a magnificent structure and people marveled at its splendor. He built a strong wall around the Temple, and above the main gate he placed an eagle, the golden emblem of Rome.

This deeply disturbed the Jews. How could a such an emblem be allowed to disgrace God's peaceful sanctuary? Didn't the Torah forbid the making of graven images? While the beauty of Herod's Temple gave him prestige abroad, it did not win him the confidence and love of his people.

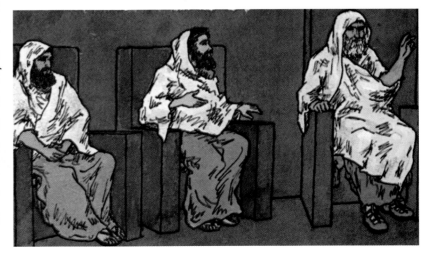

Distrusting Herod and the high priests, the people of Judea turned for leadership to the religious teachers who made up the Sanhedrin. The Sanhedrin was the institution where the laws of the Torah were interpreted in accordance with the Oral Tradition.

Students and scholars from the Jewish communities of Egypt, Babylonia, Syria, Persia, North Africa, and Rome came to Jerusalem, the center of Jewish learning, to learn Torah. When they returned home, they would teach what they had learned. In this way, they became part of the chain of scholars and sages who kept the Oral Tradition alive.

According to the Mishnah, the chain of tradition started with Moses. At Sinai, along with the Written Torah, he received an Unwritten Torah that explained and supplemented it. Moses handed the Unwritten Torah—the Oral Tradition—down to Joshua, who in turn passed it on to the elders. From them it came down to the prophets, who handed it over to the members of the Sanhedrin. Sometimes referred to as scribes, the members of the Sanhedrin were the spiritual leaders of Judea and world Jewry.

The Great Sanhedrin, which had 71 members, met in the Temple in Jerusalem. It was presided over by two leaders. One of them was the *nasi* ("prince"); the other was the *av bet din* ("presiding judge"). The two leaders in each generation are collectively referred to as the *zugot* ("pairs").

The most famous of these pairs of scholars were Hillel and Shammai.

Hillel: 1st century C.E.

HILLEL WAS A BRILLIANT YOUNG MAN who came to Judea from Babylonia. Although very poor he loved Torah learning. He earned the money to pay for admission to the lectures at the academy by cutting wood.

One cold winter's night, when he did not have the admission fee, Hillel went up to the roof of the schoolhouse and listened to the lectures through the skylight until he fell asleep. The next morning, when the academy assembled, the scholars found the hall exceptionally dark. Looking up at the skylight they saw Hillel's body blocking the sun. Touched by the young man's great devotion to learning, the teachers provided him with a scholarship.

Hillel became a famous sage. He returned to Babylonia to teach, but was invited back to Jerusalem to join the Great Sanhedrin. His wisdom and learning were recognized by Jewish scholars everywhere.

Hillel said that the way to Torah and to God was to love peace and love one's fellow human beings. He valued the unity of Israel above all, and warned his students never to set themselves apart from the community of Israel.

So greatly respected was Hillel that the office of *nasi* of the Sanhedrin became hereditary in his family. He founded a school of Torah interpretation known as Bet Hillel ("House of Hillel").

Hillel's colleague, Shammai, the *av bet din,* was a brilliant scholar who came from one of Jerusalem's wealthy noble families. He had his own ideas, and often differed with Hillel on halachic questions. While Hillel usually took the more lenient and flexible view, Shammai interpreted the law strictly. He was a pious scholar devoted to preserving the Torah and the Jewish way of life.

The difference between Hillel and Shammai is illustrated in the famous story of a pagan who tried to make fun of Judaism. He asked Shammai to explain the whole Torah within the time he could stand on one leg. Shammai became angry and chased the pagan out of his house.

Now the pagan approached Hillel and asked the same question.

With a smile Hillel calmly replied, "All of Judaism is contained in the verse in the Torah, 'You shall love your neighbor as yourself.'" The pagan was impressed and, according to the story, decided to become a Jew.

The debates between Hillel and Shammai caused a great stir. Wherever Jews studied and prayed, the teachings of Hillel and Shammai were discussed.

Despite Shammai's reputation for strictness, he believed in treating all people with friendliness.

MATCH THE COLUMNS

Herod   House of Hillel
Sanhedrin   *Nasi*
Hillel   Presiding judge
Zugot   Teachers and rabbis
Av bet din   King of Judea
Bet Hillel   Pairs

FILL IN THE BLANKS

1. _____ built two cities in honor of his Roman friends.

2. Rabbis and teachers made up the _____.

3. The *zugot* consisted of a _____ and a _____.

4. _____ was the *av bet din* of the Sanhedrin.

5. Hillel interpreted the law _____, while Shammai was much _____.

6. The members of the Sanhedrin were sometimes described as _____.

Shammai, Scribes, leniently, Herod, av bet din, nasi, Sanhedrin, stricter

ANSWER THE QUESTIONS

1. Why did the Jews distrust Herod?
2. Trace the line of the Oral Tradition starting with Moses.
3. Why was it difficult to keep track of the Oral Tradition?
4. Why didn't someone write down the decisions?
5. Hillel and Shammai had two different approaches to Jewish law. Which would you support? Why?

HILLEL AND YOU

Talmud Torah—Torah Study

Hillel wanted to include all Jews, no matter the level of their education or religious beliefs, under the tent of Judaism. He believed that in unity there was strength. One of his favorite sayings was:

Do not separate yourself from the community.

1. What is a community?
2. What is the name of the community in which you live?
3. How does a person become part of a Jewish community?
4. Is someone who goes to a different synagogue than yours a member of your Jewish community?
5. Who are the leaders in your Jewish community?
6. What Jewish activities does your community sponsor: UJA, Keren Ami, B'nai B'rith, Hadassah, etc.?
7. How is your family a part of the Jewish community?
8. How are you part of the Jewish community? Do you think it is important to have a strong Jewish community?
9. How can a strong Jewish community help the State of Israel?
10. How can a united Jewish community help on issues which concern Jews?
11. What would you do to strengthen the Jewish community in your area?

World History: 1st century C.E.

THE EARLY ROMANS WERE peasants farming the seven small hills beside the Tiber River in central Italy. They were continually attacked by powerful enemies. At first it was a case of poorly armed farmers fighting professional soldiers. But the Roman army soon became well organized. In time the Romans defeated their enemies and took control of the whole Mediterranean world. After many battles Rome carved out provinces in Spain, France, Sicily, Greece, Tunisia, and part of England. The Rhine and the Danube were its northern boundary, and much of the Middle East was its eastern boundary.

In 63 B.C.E., the Romans overran Judea and made it part of their far-flung empire. They appointed governors called procurators, who ruled the country with an iron hand. The procurators imposed high taxes and stole the gold from the Temple treasury.

The people of Judea hated the Roman yoke. In 66 C.E., led by the Zealots, they rebelled against the Romans and drove them out of Jerusalem. The Jews were elated, even though they knew that Rome would not give up easily.

Unable to accept defeat, the Romans sent a powerful army, under the command of Vespasian, to stamp out the revolt. Vespasian conquered Galilee and most of Judea, then returned home to become Rome's new emperor.

His son Titus took command of the army and in 70

C.E. began the siege of Jerusalem. It went on for several months. Despite hunger and hardship, the people of the city held out courageously. Day and night they heard the heavy thud of Roman battering rams and the noise of ballistas which shot 100-pound boulders into the city. The outer walls of Jerusalem crumbled.

On the ninth of Av, Roman troops stormed the Temple area. They climbed the walls and hurled burning torches into the city. In moments the Temple was aflame. Some of the Jewish fighters tried to escape to make a stand in another Judean fortress. A few succeeded, but most were killed or captured.

When Titus returned to Rome, the Jewish captives were paraded through the streets. They were forced to carry the golden menorah and other loot from the Temple. The Romans erected the Arch of Titus to commemorate the defeat of Judea. It can still be seen in Rome. One of the reliefs on the arch shows the Jewish captives marching in Titus's triumphal procession.

Judea was destroyed and more than a million people died in the war. Thousands were carried off into exile and slavery. Their dreams of independence was drowned in a sea of blood. The land of Israel, now called Palestine, was again ruled by a Roman governor.

Jewish communities throughout the world mourned for Judea, for Jerusalem, and above all for the Temple, which had been the spiritual center of their lives. Despite the loss of their land and their Temple, Jews continued to live in accordance with the laws of the Torah. It gave them hope and courage to face the future.

Yohanan ben Zakkai: 1st century C.E.

יוֹחָנָן בֶּן זַכַּאי

IN THE DAYS BEFORE THE SIEGE of Jerusalem, many Jews felt that Rome was sure to win. They feared that Judaism would not survive if the Romans were victorious.

But there were others who believed that the Torah itself was enough: even if land and Temple were lost, the Torah would provide a bond to unite the world's Jews and give meaning to their lives. Among those who held this view was Rabban Yohanan ben Zakkai, a scholar who had been a member of the Great Sanhedrin.

Yohanan ben Zakkai felt that Judaism would survive if the Torah lived in the hearts of the people. He taught that dignity would come not from rebellion but from observance of Jewish law.

As the Roman army neared Jerusalem, Yohanan thought of a way to preserve the Torah. He decided to start a school—an academy of Jewish learning—where the Torah could be studied and halachic questions discussed. It would be located at a distance from Jerusalem so as to be safe from the fighting.

In those days it was impossible to leave Jerusalem. With the city busily preparing for the Roman attack, the Zealots were on the look-out for traitors. Anyone who tried to leave was accused of treason.

Determined to start his school, Yohanan put himself into a coffin. His students, pretending he was dead, carried him out of Jerusalem under the watchful eye of the Zealots, supposedly to bury him.

As soon as they exited the city, Yohanan jumped out of the coffin and approached the Roman general. Vespasian was willing to meet with him, for he knew that Yohanan opposed the revolt. When Yohanan predicted that Vespasian would soon become emperor of Rome, the general was pleased and promised to grant anything he requested. This was exactly what Yohanan ben Zakkai had hoped for. He asked for permission to open a school in Yavneh, a small town on the seacoast. Vespasian agreed.

At the academy in Yavneh, the scholars continued their studies. Eventually, Yohanan formed a Sanhedrin modeled after the Great Sanhedrin of Jerusalem. Beloved and respected by everyone, he was its first *nasi*.

When the news came that Jerusalem had fallen and the Temple had been destroyed, Yohanan wept and tore his clothes in mourning. Yet he did not allow his disciples to despair.

In the aftermath of the destruction, Yohanan realized that new judges, teachers, and scholars had to be trained and ordained as in the days of the Great Sanhedrin. The scholars would have the title of rabbi, which means "master." Once ordained, each rabbi would himself become a teacher. The rabbis educated at Yavneh would be links in the great unbroken chain of teachers of the Torah.

Yohanan and those who followed him were called tannaim, meaning "repeaters" or "teachers." The period in which they were active is know as the tannaitic era. It began around the time of Hillel and ended about 200 C.E.

MATCH THE COLUMNS

1. Zealots   Patriots
2. Rabbi Yohanan   Master
3. General   Repeaters
4. Tannaim   Vespasian
5. Rabbi   ben Zakkai

FILL IN THE BLANKS

1. Roman governors were called _____.

2. The Romans conquered Judea in _____.

3. Titus and his soldiers captured Jerusalem on the _____.

4. The _____ is in Rome.

5. Rabbi Yohanan ben Zakkai was the first _____ of the Sanhedrin in _____.

**Yavneh, Procurators, ninth of Av, 63 B.C.E.,
nasi, Arch of Titus**

ANSWER THE QUESTIONS

1. Why did Yohanan put himself into a coffin?
2. Why did the Jews revolt against Rome?
3. How did the Romans commemorate the defeat of Judea?
4. What was Yohanan's plan for the survival of Judaism?
5. Do you think Yohanan ben Zakkai made the right decision to escape from Jerusalem?

YOHANAN BEN ZAKKAI AND YOU

The Torah tells us that God created the world in six days, and rested on the seventh. God created humans to rule and improve the world.

Yohanan ben Zakkai believed that we all have an obligation to make the world a better, safer, and healthier place. He said:

If you have learned much from Torah, do not claim too much credit, because you were created for this purpose.

1. According to Yohanan, for what purpose were humans created?
2. Does the Torah include all kinds of knowledge?
3. How can humans improve the world and make it a better place?
4. Name some medical discoveries that have made the world healthier.
5. Name some people who have made the world a better place.
6. Name some inventions that have made the world better.
7. Name some inventions that have made the world a dangerous place in which to live.
8. Do you have any suggestions for making the world happier and safer?
9. As a grown-up, how would you improve the world?
10. Which organizations would you join?

World History: 2nd century C.E.

FOLLOWING THE DESTRUCTION of Jerusalem in 70 C.E., the Romans allowed Judea a period of peace and reconstruction. However, conditions changed when Emperor Hadrian decided to rebuild Jerusalem.

Hadrian visited the city and personally supervised the building projects. On the site of the Holy Temple he built an altar dedicated to the god Jupiter. He also issued laws which made it difficult to practice Judaism.

Many Jews wanted to rebel against Rome and once more fight for freedom. The spirit of revolt even spread to the academy, where the scholars usually favored peace. Rabbi Akiba was one of the leaders who wanted to rebel against Rome.

By the time Hadrian became emperor, Akiba was very old. When he heard about Simon Bar Kozeba, a young man who was organizing a guerilla force to fight the Romans, Akiba felt that the time was at hand. He gave Bar Kozeba his support and renamed him Simon Bar Kochba, meaning "Son of a Star." Akiba believed that Bar Kochba might actually be the Messiah, sent by God to restore the freedom of the Jewish people.

The insurrection began in 132 C.E. and lasted for three and one-half years. Roman patrols were ambushed and Roman supplies were captured. Hadrian sent an army

to support the Palestine garrison, but his troops were defeated. Bar Kochba marched and lived with his men, sharing all their hardships. He insisted on leading them himself. As a result, his men were devoted to him and would do almost anything he commanded.

Bar Kochba went from victory to victory, and the Roman army retreated into Syria. The victorious Jewish army entered Jerusalem. Under Bar Kochba's leadership, Judea enjoyed two years of independence.

Hadrian now came to Judea in person, bringing reinforcements. Bar Kochba and his brave fighters made a final stand in the mountain fortress of Betar, near Jerusalem. The Jewish soldiers fought desperately, but in the end Betar fell.

Judea was laid waste and completely destroyed. Hundreds of thousands of Jews were killed, and just as many were sold into slavery.

In Jerusalem, as was their custom, the Romans cleared away the rubble and plowed up the ground. On the site they built the new city Hadrian had planned, a heathen city with temples for the worship of Roman gods. It was called Aelia Capitolina.

The Romans knew that Judaism was the source of the Jewish people's strength. They concluded that if the religious leaders were eliminated, the ordinary people would yield to Roman authority. Accordingly, soldiers hunted down the most important leaders.

Rabbi Simeon bar Yochai had to go into hiding. Rabbi Akiba was arrested and condemned to be skinned alive. With his last breath the saintly hero proclaimed the words of the Shema, "Hear, O Israel, the Lord is our God, the Lord is One."

Rabbi Akiba: 40–135 C.E.

RABBI AKIBA WAS the most outstanding of the many scholars and rabbis who taught at Yavneh. As a young man he had been an uneducated shepherd. Then he had married Rachel, the daughter of his wealthy master. Over the years she made many sacrifices to enable him to fulfill his ambition of learning Torah.

When Akiba gave up being a shepherd and left home to attend the academy, Rachel cut off her hair and sold it to a wig merchant in order to pay for his tuition.

Thanks to Rachel's sacrifices, Akiba was able to attend the academy of Eliezer and Joshua, who were carrying on the work of Yohanan ben Zakkai. Akiba was not only a great scholar but a great teacher. Students flocked to the lectures at his academy at Bnei Brak.

Rabbi Akiba initiated one of the most important projects in the history of Jewish law. With the aid of his colleagues, he set about organizing the vast body of halachot, discussions, and legal cases comprising the Oral Tradition. Akiba did not put all of this down in writing, for it was not yet the custom to do so. However, he originated the idea of classifying the material by subject.

Thanks to this system, which is known as the Mishnah of Rabbi Akiba, scholars found it much easier to locate important information.

Akiba was away studying for twenty-four years. When he finally returned, he was recognized as a great scholar, and was respected by thousands of students. The people crowded around to see the great scholar. Among them was an old man dressed in fine clothing but with a sorrowful face.

"Many years ago," he said to Akiba, "I made a vow. Now I am old, and do not have many years left. I regret my vow and would like to know if I can be released from it."

"What was the vow?" asked Rabbi Akiba.

"When my daughter angered me by marrying a poor shepherd," said the man, "I swore I would never speak to her or help her in any way."

"Why did you make the vow?" asked Rabbi Akiba.

"Because he was an ignorant man, who could not even read or write," said the old man.

"Vows can easily be nullified," said Akiba.

"But this one was made because of a certain condition," said the old man.

"If the condition has changed, the vow need no longer be kept," said Akiba. "You may consider your vow null and void, because I am that same ignorant shepherd."

Rachel's father was delighted to learn that his son-in-law was now a distinguished scholar.

Akiba never failed to give credit to Rachel for his achievements. When asked who was really a rich man, he always answered, "He who has a good wife."

Rabbi Akiba ben Joseph was the most respected and beloved of the talmudic sages. Most of the scholars of the following generations were his disciples. His decisions were widely accepted, and later talmudists declared that his opinions must be granted preference over all others. Because of the great importance of the Mishnah of Rabbi Akiba, the rabbis declared that he had kept the Torah from disappearing.

MATCH THE COLUMNS

1. Destruction of
   Jerusalem   Prince
2. Trajan   Mishnah
3. Jerusalem   70 C.E.
4. Rabbi Akiba   Roman Emperor
5. *Nasi*   Aelia Capitolina

FILL IN THE BLANKS

1. In 98 C.E. _____ became emperor of _____.

2. Bar Kochba means "Son of a _____."

3. Rabbi Akiba believed that Simon Bar Kochba was
   the _____.

4. Bar Kochba and his soldiers made their last stand in the
   fortress of _____.

5. Rabbi Akiba began to classify and organize the _____.

Betar, Messiah, Rome, Star, Trajan, Oral Tradition

ANSWER THE QUESTIONS

1. Why did the Jews rebel against Rome?
2. Why did the Romans decide to destroy Jerusalem?
3. Why did the Romans eliminate the religious leaders?
4. How did Rachel help Akiba get an education?
5. Why did Rachel's father want to break his vow?
6. How did Rabbi Akiba die?

RABBI AKIBA AND YOU

The Hebrew word *tzedakah* comes from *tzedek,* meaning "justice." The ancient rabbis believed that helping people in need was a religious duty and an act of justice.

Today, we apply the word tzedakah to all sorts of acts of charity, such as giving money to help a worthy cause or a person in need. According to the Torah, every person's possessions—even yours—really belong to God. Therefore, when you help someone in need, you are merely distributing God's money, food, clothing. Listen to Rabbi Akiba's question and answer:

Question: *What is the best offering to God?*
Answer: *Charity to His children.*

1. Who are God's children?
2. What did Rabbi Akiba mean by the phrase "offering to God"?
3. Are you one of God's children? Are your father and mother? Your brothers and sisters?
4. Are your teachers in public school or religious school God's children?
5. Do you have to be Jewish to be one of God's children?
6. Is giving any kind of charity considered an offering to God?
7. Do you have to be Jewish to bring an offering to God?
8. Do you have to be an adult to bring an offering to God?
9. What is your favorite charity?
10. Is it possible to bring an offering without money? Explain.
11. Is doing a mitzvah considered an offering?
12. Is Rabbi Akiba's statement as true today as it was thousands of years ago?
13. Is visiting an old-age home an act of tzedakah?
14. Is helping a sick or old person by doing an errand an act of tzedakah?
15. Can you think of other ways of doing mitzvot?

World History: 2nd century C.E.

AFTER THE DEFEAT of Bar Kochba in 135 C.E., the Jewish population of Palestine sharply decreased. A huge number had been killed in the revolt or sold into slavery in other lands. Many of those who remained alive fled the Roman sword to safer parts of the world. After a while, however, a new administration in Rome made life safer for the Jews who still lived in their traditional homeland.

In 138, Emperor Antoninus Pius granted permission to reopen the schools and reestablish the Bet Din (Jewish court). During his reign Roman rule was much less harsh. The rabbis who had hidden from the Romans were now able to resume their leadership roles.

With the end of the persecutions in Palestine, a new religious center was founded in the town of Usha. Rabbi Judah ben Ilai, a student of Rabbi Akiba, established an academy there. Once again the Sanhedrin was reestablished and a *nasi* was chosen as the spiritual head of the Jewish community.

The new Sanhedrin reopened schools and synagogues throughout the land. It began to ordain rabbis and set up schools where children were taught Hebrew and learned their heritage. Voluntary taxes were collected to support religious and educational institutions and help the poor.

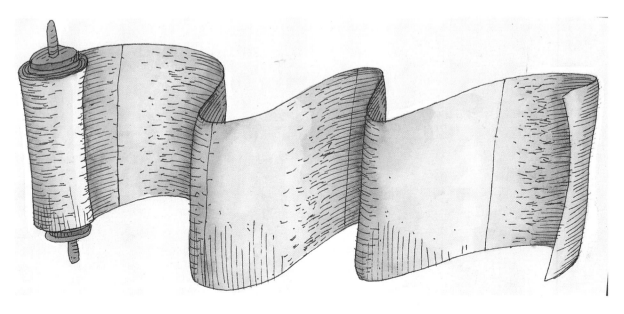

Until this time the legal decisions of the sages had not been written down. Over the centuries a huge body of material had accumulated, known as the Oral Tradition. The Oral Tradition explained what the Written Torah meant. It consisted of lectures, questions and answers, legal opinions, discussions by the sages, and much more.

Although the Mishnah of Rabbi Akiba was an invaluable first step in systematically organizing this vast collection, there was still the problem of remembering it and handing it on. Every year, as more material accumulated, the problem became more serious. As a result, there was a great fear that the Oral Tradition and the work of the previous generations would be lost.

The task of preserving it fell to the genius of Rabbi Judah HaNasi—Judah the Prince.

Judah HaNasi: 2nd century C.E.

JUDAH THE PRINCE SUCCEEDED his father, Simon, who had become *nasi* after the second revolt in 132 C.E. He held the office for almost 50 years.

An outstanding scholar, Judah HaNasi moved the Sanhedrin and the academy to Beth She'arim, and later to Sepphoris. As *nasi* he had the sole authority to ordain rabbis and judges even for posts in other countries.

In Judah HaNasi's time, most Jews, even in the land of Israel, spoke Aramaic. Judah was greatly concerned about the survival of Hebrew. He wanted it to be a living language, used every day in Jewish homes. To set an example, he and his household spoke only Hebrew. It was said that Judah's servants spoke better Hebrew than many scholars. Judah used Hebrew when he compiled his great law code, the Mishnah.

Judah's love of the Torah and of Hebrew went hand in hand with wide cultural interests. He knew several languages and was learned in many subjects. He had many non-Jewish friends, including Marcus Aurelius (121–180 C.E.), a Roman emperor who was interested in philosophy.

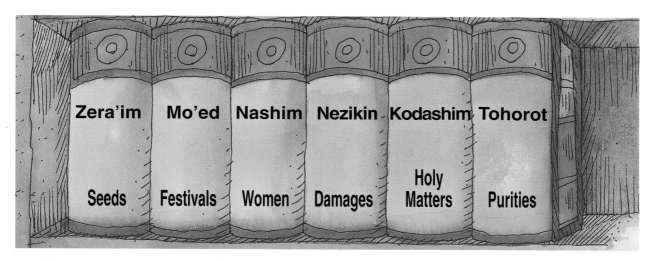

The academy established by Rabbi Judah the Prince was a great success. Students from Babylonia and other faraway places came there to study. He used to say, "I have learned much from my teachers, more from my colleagues, but most of all from my students." Judah HaNasi gave freely of his wealth to needy students and scholars and to the poor of the land.

The Oral Tradition had grown so big that scholars could not possibly remember all of it. The rabbis wisely decided that it was time to write everything down if the Oral Tradition was to survive. Judah set to work on the great task. The entire Oral Tradition was logically arranged according to subject. Around 200 C.E. it was put into written form that would ensure its survival.

The work that resulted from these efforts is called the Mishnah. It consists of six sections called orders (*sedarim*), each of which is subdivided into several tractates (*massechtot*). Altogether, there are 63 tractates. The Mishnah is written in Hebrew. Several centuries later it became the basis for the vast encyclopedia of Jewish law and lore known as the Talmud.

When Rabbi Judah the Prince died, around 220 C.E., he was mourned deeply by his friends, colleagues, and students. He was one of those rare men who embodied the spirit of a kind father for an entire people. "Not since Moses," the people said, "has there been a man like Judah, who so combined leadership with Torah." Judah's body was brought to burial at Beth She'arim. Everyone seemed to feel that a great era of Jewish history had come to an end.

With the death of Judah HaNasi the tannaitic period ended. He is traditionally regarded as the last of the tannaim (teachers).

MATCH THE COLUMNS

1. Bet Din   Prince
2. Tannaim   *Perakim*
3. *nasi*   Jewish Court
4. Oral Tradition   *Massechtot*
5. Tractates   Teachers
6. Chapters   Mishnah

FILL IN THE BLANKS

1. The Babylonian Talmud is divided into 63 _____.

2. Rabbi Judah ben Ilai established a _____ in the town of Usha.

3. Rabbi Akiba began to write down the _____.

4. _____ is regarded as the last of the _____.

5. In Judah's time most Jews spoke _____.

6. The Mishnah is written in _____.

**tannaim, Aramaic, Hebrew, academy, tractates,
Judah HaNasi, Mishnah**

ANSWER THE QUESTIONS

1. Why was it necessary to develop religious institutions which could function in a foreign country?
2. Why did the rabbis decide to write down and keep track of the Oral Tradition?
3. Why did Judah try to preserve the Hebrew language?
4. What was the tannaitic age?

JUDAH HANASI AND YOU

Judah HaNasi said: *"I have learned much from my teachers, more from my colleagues, but most of all from my students."*

1. Who were Judah's teachers?
2. What did Judah learn from his teachers?
3. What is a colleague?
4. How can a person learn from a colleague?
5. Does a colleague discuss a problem, debate, or ask questions?
6. After years of study, Judah finally became a teacher. From Judah's statement, how do you think he treated his students?
7. Did he respect their opinions and encourage them?
8. How could students teach anything to a genius like Judah HaNasi?
9. Who are your teachers in Hebrew school?
10. What are they trying to teach you?
11. What can you learn from your colleagues (classmates) as you discuss, debate, and ask questions?
12. When you become an adult and assume a position of authority, or become a teacher or a craftsman, will you adopt Judah's attitude toward your colleagues? Your employees? Your students? Your children?
13. Is it a good idea to have patience, as Judah HaNasi did, to listen and to learn from others?
14. Is it a good idea to speak less and listen more?

BABYLONIA WAS A RICH, FERTILE COUNTRY situated between the Tigris and Euphrates rivers. Jews had lived there for hundreds of years, dating back to the exile following Nebuchadnezzar's capture of Jerusalem in the 6th century B.C.E. At the time of the Second Temple, more Jews lived in Babylonia than in Judea.

The Babylonian Jewish community was rich and prosperous. It generously contributed toward the rebuilding of Palestine after the return from the exile. For centuries, Jews in every part of Babylonia voluntarily paid a Temple tax for this purpose which was collected in Nehardea and sent to Judea.

Some of the Babylonian Jews lived on the great fertile plains, and were farmers and cattle-ranchers. Others worked in the cities as craftsmen, merchants, bankers, and traders. The Jews of Babylonia maintained their own synagogues, houses of study, and courts, although they turned for guidance to the Great Sanhedrin in Jerusalem.

Like Jews everywhere, the Jews of Babylonia regarded Palestine as the spiritual center of Judaism. Babylonian students, among them the great Hillel, flocked to Jerusalem to study Torah. After the destruction of the Second Temple, Babylonian Jews studied with the tannaim at the academies in Yavneh, Tiberias, and Sepphoris.

In Roman times, Babylonia was ruled by the Parthians, who were tolerant of the Jews in their land. After the two revolts, refugees from Judea streamed into Parthia's Babylonian provinces to begin a new life there. Thus the Jewish community of Babylonia grew in numbers and strength.

Babylonian Jewry was headed by an official called the *resh galuta* ("leader of the exile" or "exilarch"). The exilarch ruled over all the Jewish communities in Babylonia. He collected taxes for the government as well as the taxes which the Jews levied on themselves to support their communal institutions.

The exilarch was the highest authority in the Jewish courts of justice and in all the affairs of the Babylonian Jewish community. When his carriage appeared on the streets, a runner would announce his coming. The Jews were proud of the exilarch, and showed him great respect.

Because there was often a lack of able leaders and teachers, Jewish educational and legal institutions in Babylonia eventually began to deteriorate. As a result, talented students from Babylonia went to study in the academies in Palestine, as Hillel had done centuries earlier. Two of these young Babylonians, Abba Arikha and Samuel, were among the most gifted of Judah HaNasi's students.

אַבָּא אֲרִיכָא (רַב)

Abba Arikha: 3rd century C.E.

In the early centuries, Babylonian Jewry's brightest young men went to study in Palestine. One of these young Babylonians, Abba Arikha ("Abba the Tall"), was among the most gifted of Judah HaNasi's students. Because of his brilliance, Abba Arikha is usually known simply as Rav, meaning "Master." The word *rav* eventually became the title of all ordained rabbis.

When Rav returned to Babylonia, he brought with him a copy of the newly composed Mishnah. The exilarch appointed him inspector of markets and of weights and measures for the Jewish communities of Babylonia. As he journeyed through the land, Rav saw how slack the people's spiritual life had become. He began to reorganize the schools and synagogues.

Eventually, Rav was appointed head of the academy at Nehardea, but he declined this post so that it could be given to another gifted student of Judah HaNasi, his colleague Mar Samuel, also known as Samuel Yarhina'ah ("Samuel the Astronomer").

Rav went on to found an academy of his own in Sura, near the city of Pumpeditha. His new school attracted many scholars and students.

Rav instituted a revolutionary new plan of study, open to anyone who wanted to take advantage of it. Every year, during the months of Adar (March–April) and Elul (September), when the farmers could be spared from their work and when artisans and merchants

could take a rest during their slack season, Rav would give a special course in Jewish law. These months were called the months of Kallah ("Assembly").

During the Kallah months and the weeks preceding the holidays, people would stream into Sura from all the provinces to attend the popular courses at the academy. A thirst for learning took hold of Babylonian Jewry. Throughout the land synagogues and schoolhouses were improved and Jews met in great numbers to study and learn.

With the help of the Mishnah, Babylonian scholars were able to apply the Torah's teachings to life in exile. By introducing the Mishnah to their students, Rav and Samuel succeeded in making the Torah a living guide that enabled the Jews of Babylonia to deal with the many problems they faced.

Samuel and Rav remained close friends and collaborators throughout their lives. Together, they revised the Siddur (prayerbook). Rav wrote the beautiful Alenu prayer for Rosh Hashanah; it is still part of our daily service. Samuel wrote a shorter version of the Shemoneh Esreh (Amidah)—the Eighteen Benedictions.

Samuel's last years were darkened by trouble. In 226 C.E., the Parthians were overthrown by the Persians. The new rulers of Babylonia were Zoroastrians. Their priests tried to force this religion on all the inhabitants of the territories they had conquered. Since the Jews were not willing to accept Zoroastrianism, a time of persecution began.

After Samuel's death, Nehardea was plundered by desert raiders. It never regained its former importance. Now the main centers of Jewish learning shifted to Sura and Pumpeditha.

MATCH THE COLUMNS

1. Palestine   Leader in exile
2. Abba Arikha   River
3. *Resh galuta*   Spiritual center
4. Euphrates   Rav

FILL IN THE BLANKS

1. During the months of _____, Jews would stream into Sura.

2. _____ and _____ remained close friends all their lives.

3. The _____ priests tried to force their religion onto the Jews.

4. _____ was situated between the Tigris and the Euphrates.

5. The _____ ruled over all the Jewish communities in _____.

Babylonia, Samuel, Kallah, Rav, Zoroastrian, exilarch, Babylonia

ANSWER THE QUESTIONS

1. Why did the Jews of Babylonia regard Palestine as the spiritual center of Judaism?
2. Who ruled Babylonia in Roman times?
3. Why did the Jewish community in Babylon continue to grow?
4. How did Rav spread Jewish learning?
5. What text helped apply Torah teachings to the exiles?
6. What event brought trouble to Samuel's last years?
7. What became the title of ordained rabbis?

ABBA ARIKHA AND YOU

Rav was a highly respected scholar in the Babylonian community. Because of his ability, the exilarch appointed him market commissioner (*egoranomos*). He supervised market cleanliness, weights and measures, and the treatment of the livestock.

In this capacity Rav was in close contact with the farmers and the cattle-raisers. He saw how animals were treated and was concerned about their welfare.

Preventing cruelty to animals is called *tzar ba'alei chayyim*. The treatment of animals is mentioned in the Fourth Commandment: "The seventh day is a Sabbath to the Lord your God: you shall not do any work, you, your sons, or your daughters; your oxen, your donkeys, or any of your cattle."

There are other Torah laws that protect the welfare of animals. The laws of kashrut regulate the way animals are slaughtered, so as to cause them a minimum of pain. Because animals had to be slaughtered in a specific way, the hunting and killing of animals was denounced as cruel.

In one of his lectures, Rav said:
Do not eat until you have fed your animals.

1. Why was Rav concerned about the welfare of animals?
2. Are animals God's creations?
3. Can animals complain about the way they are treated?
4. How can hunting an animal be cruel and painful?
5. Are there any organizations concerned with the welfare of animals?
6. Do you own a pet or know someone who owns one?
7. How do you or they treat their animals?
8. Do you think Rav's advice is applicable today?
9. Do you follow Rav's advice with regard to your pets?

World History: 7th century C.E.

AN ARAB NAMED MOHAMMED proclaimed a new religion and called it Islam, meaning "submission" to the will of God. After his death in 632 C.E., he was succeeded by Caliph Abu Bakr and then by Caliph Omar.

Omar and his army of Bedouin horsemen conquered Egypt, Palestine, Syria, and Persia, spreading the faith of Islam to all of these lands. In 638 Omar captured Jerusalem and established a Moslem sanctuary there. Once again Jews were permitted to enter the city and to pray at the Western Wall. Soon there was a small Jewish community in Jerusalem.

Although Jewish life in Palestine revived after the Moslem conquest, Babylonia remained the main center of world Jewry. After the Arabs conquered Babylonia in 660, the situation rapidly improved. The persecution by the Zoroastrians came to an end. The schools of Sura and Pumpeditha reopened and were presided over by the geonim.

Under the Arabs, the Jewish community regained its autonomy. It was once again led by the exilarch, who now was authorized to collect taxes both for the caliph and for the Jewish community. The gaonim were given the right to select the exilarch, but their choice had to be approved by the caliph.

Whenever Jews anywhere were in doubt on questions of Jewish law, they would send messengers to the geonim in Babylonia. The Babylonian scholars sent their answers and legal decisions in clear, concise letters known as *teshuvot* (responsa). Ever since, decisions on halachic questions by Jewish scholars have been set down in accordance with the form used in the gaonic responsa. Nowadays responsa are still written by prominent rabbis who are experts on the halachah.

The gaonic period extended from the 7th to the 11th century. During this era the geonim sent teachers to acquaint Jews in far-off communities with developments in Sura and Pumpeditha, and to teach the Talmud.

By this means, knowledge of the Talmud was spread far and wide, and a bond was established among the many groups that made up world Jewry. Jewish communities thousands of miles away in Spain learned Talmud under teachers from Babylonia and sent teshuvot to the Babylonian academies.

Over the centuries of exile, Jews were becoming confused and divided by many issues. Some doubted their religion. Others believed in magic, or waited for the Messiah, or refused to accept the authority of the gaonim. There was no strong leader to guide them in this time of turmoil and confusion. Fortunately, in the midst of the crisis, a leader stepped forward who was not afraid to battle for traditional Judaism. That man was Saadia Gaon.

Saadia Gaon: 882–942 C.E.

SAADIA GAON WAS A SCHOLAR, an author, and the leader of Babylonian Jewry. His achievements marked him as one of the most important personalities of the period. Saadia was born in 882 in a village in Egypt. Even as a young man his brilliance was apparent. He mastered the entire range of Jewish literature and also studied Moslem literary and scientific writings.

During Saadia's lifetime, traditional Judaism was faced with the challenge posed by the Karaites, a breakaway sect that refused to accept the Talmud and the authority of the rabbis.

The Karaites rejected the system of Jewish law that had developed since the time of the Mishnah. Instead they advocated a form of Judaism based solely on what was written in the Torah. Their name in Hebrew, B'nai Mikra ("people of the Bible"), reflects their strict emphasis on the Written Torah as opposed to the Oral Tradition.

Karaism met with considerable success at first, because many Jews found talmudic Judaism difficult to understand. In abandoning the Talmud, the Karaites failed to recognize that the talmudic rules were designed to make life easier. By sticking to the literal text of the Torah, they made things more difficult for themselves.

The Torah, for instance, says that you may not have a fire in your house on Shabbat. The Karaites observed this to the letter. Thus, on

the Sabbath, they had no light or heat and were only able to eat cold food. The rabbinic rules, however, permitted keeping a fire burning from before Shabbat in order to prevent such discomforts. The Karaites also believed that one had to stay home on Shabbat. Rabbinic interpretation of the Torah forbade travel, but one was permitted to attend services in the synagogue, take a walk, and visit. All these activities make Shabbat more pleasant and more meaningful.

Saadia Gaon recognized the threat that Karaism posed to rabbinic Judaism. By exposing the weaknesses of Karaism, Saadia restored the unity of world Jewry.

Eventually, Saadia settled in Babylonia, where he became the gaon (head) of the yeshiva in Sura. Saadia felt that the best way to improve the quality of Jewish learning was by applying the methods of science and philosophy. Since there were as yet no Hebrew grammars or Bible dictionaries, he set to work to provide some of these important tools.

Saadia was an accomplished poet in both Arabic and Hebrew. He translated the Bible into Arabic and put together one of the first Jewish prayerbooks. It was called the Siddur, meaning "order" (of prayer).

Saadia's Siddur was a very important achievement. Until this time the synagogue service had no fixed order or content. Now a more or less standardized service came into use among Jews everywhere.

In the days of Saadia Gaon, the prestige and power of the geonim reached their high point. Saadia Gaon died at the age of 60. In his relatively short life his talent and personality made him one of the dominant figures in the development of Judaism and its literature.

After the death of the great master, the importance of the Babylonian schools diminished, and with it the influence of the geonim.

MATCH THE COLUMNS

1. Siddur
2. Saadia
3. *Teshuvot*
4. Sura
5. Karaites

Pumpeditha
Order
B'nai Mikra
Gaon
Responsa

FILL IN THE BLANKS

1. The _____ was authorized to collect taxes for the Jewish community.

2. The _____ had the right to select the exilarch.

3. The Babylonian scholars sent _____ to legal questions.

4. Today, responsa are written by rabbis who are experts on _____.

5. Saadia Gaon was the head of the _____ in Sura.

6. Saadia Gaon translated the _____ into _____.

Siddur, exilarch, responsa, Arabic, yeshiva, halachah, caliph

ANSWER THE QUESTIONS

1. What was the difference between Karaism and rabbinic Judaism?
2. How did Saadia Gaon improve the traditional method of teaching?
3. What are responsa?
4. How did the gaonin establish a bond with world Jewry?

SAADIA GAON AND YOU
Hochmah—Wisdom

You are not born with wisdom. This quality is acquired from your parents, teachers, education, and life experience. All of these factors help you to acquire wisdom.

One of Saadia Gaon's greatest works was the *Sefer Emunot Ve-Deot* ("Book of Beliefs and Opinions"), which explains Judaism's central beliefs and ideas. Written in Arabic, it was helpful to the many Jews in Moslem countries who no longer spoke or read Hebrew. In a period of challenging ideas and religious confusion, Saadia's clear thinking provided answers to many Jews who needed guidance. In this book, Saadia Gaon wrote:

Many people have gotten lost and failed to gain wisdom. Some did not know which road to take, others took the right road but did not travel far enough.

1. What did Saadia mean by "getting lost" and "not traveling far enough"? What kind of road was he talking about?
2. How far does a person have to travel before gaining wisdom?
3. What is your definition of wisdom?
4. How can you judge whether you are on the right road?
5. Do you have to travel a set distance, or does it vary from person to person?
6. Do you know anybody who has wisdom? Can that person tell you how to gain wisdom?
7. What do you have to do to reach the end of the wisdom road?
8. Is there ever an end to the wisdom road?
9. In your own words, describe what Saadia is telling you?
10. Does Saadia's statement have any meaning for you today?
11. How can Saadia's advice help you plan your education and your career?

World History: 11th–12th century C.E.

CHRISTIAN EUROPE FELT THREATENED by the rise of Islam and was concerned about the Moslem control of Jerusalem. To Christians as to Jews, Palestine was the Holy Land. It was holy because Jesus, the father of their faith, had lived and preached there.

In 1095, a church council met in France and announced the First Crusade. This was to be a holy war to liberate Palestine from the Moslem unbelievers. The Crusader armies assembled to march to the Holy Land. Inflammatory sermons by the clergy raised the anger of the Crusaders against aliens and infidels.

Throughout the 11th century, the Jewish communities of the Rhineland in western Germany had been great centers of rabbinic scholarship. The yeshivot in the cities of Mainz, Worms, and Cologne had been crowded with hundreds of young and old Talmud students.

Unfortunately, these cities were on the line of march of the Crusaders, and their Jewish inhabitants became the first victims of the "Holy War." In May 1096, the soldiers of the First Crusade killed or forcibly converted the Jews of Worms, Mainz, and Cologne. The destruction of these centers of learning increased the importance of Rashi's yeshiva in France. Rashi and his students assumed the leadership in Jewish scholarship. Like lights glowing in the darkness, they kept the flame of Jewish learning alight.

רַבִּי שְׁלֹמֹה בֶּן יִצְחָק (רַשִׁ"י)
Rabbi Solomon ben Itzhak: 1040–1105

DESPITE THE GRIM SITUATION in the Middle Ages, Jewish scholarship was assured by the birth of a child in the year 1040 in the French city of Troyes. This child was destined to become the most popular and important figure in Ashkenazic rabbinic Judaism—Rabbi Solomon ben Itzhak, popularly know as *Rashi*.

As a young man, Rashi studied at the academy in Worms, Germany. The parents and relatives of many of the students at the academy were engaged in international trade. They discussed their journeys in faraway lands with their children. In this way the students obtained a great deal of knowhow about business, agriculture, manufacturing and crafts, foreign countries, modes of travel, and other matters.

Rashi's knowledge of the world was greatly enriched by what he learned from his fellow students. On his return to Troyes, he earned his living from his vineyards, but devoted most of his time to teaching and writing.

When the Holocaust of 1096—the First Crusade—destroyed the yeshivot of the Rhineland, Rashi's tiny yeshiva became the most important center for talmudic study in Germany and France.

Before long Rashi's influence spread throughout the Jewish world. Students flocked to his yeshiva, and scholars everywhere corresponded with him, asking his advice on questions that confused them.

Rashi was the first commentator to help the ordinary Jew understand biblical and talmudic texts. His Torah commentary made it possible for everyone, even those who were not full-time scholars, to study the Bible with understanding.

There are two aspects to most biblical passages: the *peshat,* the simple, plain meaning, and the *derash,* the poetic meaning. In writing his commentary, Rashi first looked for the *peshat,* searching the body of Jewish literature to see what earlier scholars had suggested; if he couldn't find a satisfactory *peshat* meaning, he took the *derash* route and looked for a fanciful explanation.

In his commentary, Rashi quotes every biblical word or phrase that requires explanation, and then briefly clarifies it by reference to the Jewish sources or on the basis of his own knowledge. Since he lived in France, and his students were all familiar with the language of the country, he sometimes used French words in order to make the Bible's meaning as clear as possible. When he uses a French word he prefaces it with the phrase *b'laaz,* meaning "in a foreign tongue." It was very time-consuming to write the regular Hebrew alefbet. So Rashi used the cursive script that was much easier and faster to wrtie. Most of the early commentaries of the Torah and the Talmud are printed in Rashi script.

In addition to his commentary on the Torah, Rashi produced a commentary on the Talmud. His genius lay in his ability to simplify and edit the explanations offered by generations of scholars.

Rashi's work of commenting on the Bible and Talmud was continued by his grandsons. The most prominent of them were Rabbi Shmuel ben Meir (1080–1174), known as Rashbam, and Rabbi Jacob ben Meir (1100–1171), known as Rabbenu Tam. Rashi's daughters were also famous for their great wisdom and knowledge.

THE RASHI SCRIPT					
Mem Sofit	ם	ם	Alef	א	ƒ
Nun	נ	ﬤ	Beit	ב	ﬤ
Nun Sofit	ן	ן	Gimel	ג	ﬤ
Samech	ס	ﬤ	Daled	ד	ﬤ
Ayin	ע	ﬤ	Hay	ה	ﬤ
Fay	פ	ﬤ	Vav	ו	ﬤ
Fay Sofit	ף	�	Zayin	ז	ﬤ
Tzadi	צ	ﬤ	Chet	ח	ﬤ
Tzadi Sofit	ץ	ﬤ	Tet	ט	ﬤ
Quf	ק	ﬤ	Yud	י	ﬤ
Resh	ר	ﬤ	Khaf	כ	ﬤ
Sin	ש	ﬤ	Khaf Sofit	ך	ﬤ
Tav	ת	ﬤ	Lamed	ל	ﬤ

MATCH THE COLUMNS

1. Mohammed   Plain
2. Palestine   Rashi
3. Crusaders   Foreign tongue
4. Solomon ben Itzhak   Holy War
5. *Peshat*   Islam
6. *b'laaz*   Holy Land

FILL IN THE BLANKS

1. In 638 C.E. Omar conquered _____.

2. _____ yeshiva was in Troyes.

3. Rashi earned his living from his _____.

4. Rashi mostly used the _____ explanations in his commentaries.

5. Rashi wrote commentaries on the Bible and on the _____.

Talmud, vineyards, Palestine, peshat, Rashi's

ANSWER THE QUESTIONS

1. What is the difference between *peshat* and *derash*?
2. Why were Rashi's commentaries popular?
3. Why did Christians feel threatened by the rise of Islam?
4. Why was Rashi's yeshiva important for the continuation of Franco-German scholarship?
5. How did Rashi acquire his knowledge about the world outside of Troyes?

RASHI AND YOU

The Shema says,
"You shall love the Lord your God . . . with all your might."

Rashi's commentary on the Torah explains this phrase.

Rashi says:
> **"Your might** *refers to all of your possessions. There are people who value their possessions more than they value themselves."*

He also says:
> **"With all your might** *refers to everything God has given you, whether with goods or with poverty, with good or with evil, even in sadness, to continue to serve God."*

1. With what does Rashi equate possessions?
2. How can money and possessions become might?
3. Can might do good things?
4. Can it do bad things?
5. Name some bad and good things that might can do.
6. Suppose you become sick or bankrupt; should you continue to use your possessions to do good?
7. You are still a kid, but you have some possessions. How can you do good with them?
8. Your mind, your skills, and your health are your possessions. How can you use them to do good?
9. Do you have any special skills, such as singing, playing an instrument, telling jokes, doing card tricks, dunking a basketball, etc.? How can you use your skills to do good?
10. What do you think of Rashi's interpretations?
11. Can you think of your own interpretations?

World History: 8th–12th century

THE EVERYDAY LANGUAGE OF THE JEWS of North Africa was Arabic. In North Africa, as in most other Moslem lands, learning, science, and art flourished, and many Jews contributed to the study of astronomy, medicine, and mathematics. Jewish poets wrote beautiful verses in Arabic.

In the 8th century the Moors of North Africa prepared to sail across the Mediterranean to conquer Spain. In 711, the Moorish general Tarik crossed the Straits of Gibraltar, and within four years all of Spain was under Moslem domination.

Many Jews left North Africa to follow the conquering Moorish armies to Spain. The old Jewish communities of Spain were greatly influenced by these Arabic-speaking Jews, who already knew the freedom of the Arab world.

In 755, the city of Cordova, in the south of Spain, became the capital of the Moorish caliphate. Under its Arab rulers, Spain became a land of beautiful architecture, a land of learning and science, poetry and music. With the coming of the Moors, a new era of freedom began in Spain. The country's populace now consisted of people from four different groups: the Moorish conquerors, people of the old Spanish stock who had been in Spain before the coming of the

Visigoths in Roman times, Christian Visigoths, and a small minority of Jews.

The north of Spain was divided into several small Christian kingdoms. But the south of Spain, called Andalusia by the Arabs, was in the hands of the Moslems.

The Moslem rulers of Spain were tolerant and wanted all their subjects to participate in the life of the new commonwealth. Although the language of the land was Arabic, and Islam was the religion of the court, all the people of Andalusia enjoyed relatively equal opportunities regardless of religion. A golden age had dawned for the Jews in Spain. Schools of Jewish learning were founded, especially in Cordova, which had the good fortune to be visited by scholars from Babylonia. The Babylonian teachers introduced the Babylonian method of learning and interpreting the halachah.

The Jews of Spain entered many professions. They worked as farmers and vintners, goldsmiths, sailors, and shoemakers. Spanish Jews also entered the sciences, becoming astronomers and mathematicians.

During the Golden Age (10th–12th century C.E.) Jewish life was relatively free, although the Moslems insisted on second-class citizenship (*dhimma*) remaining in force. Non-Moslems were called *dhimmis*, and had to pay a poll tax and promise not to insult Islam. The Jews fulfilled two important functions: as a link between the Moslems and the Christians, and as functionaries that released Moslems from military service.

Because of their contacts, both religious and commercial, in countries as far off as Babylonia, many Jews were able to speak several languages. This enabled them to act as ambassadors and interpreters for the Moorish caliphs, performing commercial and diplomatic missions of many kinds.

Judah Halevi: 1075–1141

TO THIS DAY, JUDAH HALEVI is the most beloved of the Spanish-Jewish poets. Born in Toledo, Halevi studied at the academy in Lucena, where he received an intensive Hebrew education. A scholar of Arabic literature, he was learned in astronomy and mathematics and was a skilled physician.

Eventually Judah returned to Toledo to practice medicine. Though he was one of the most famous physicians of his day, he felt that he was only a humble assistant to God, the true healer. He wrote:

My medicines are of You, and tell of Your art—good or evil, strong or weak. The choice is in Your hands, not in mine: Knowledge of all things is Yours. I do not heal with the power in me, but only through the healing sent from You.

Although his medical career kept him busy, Judah wrote hundreds of poems of prayer and thanksgiving, many of which are included in the Siddur. His daughter was the light of his life, and she became as learned as Rashi's daughters. When she had a son, she named him in honor of his famous grandfather.

As Judah Halevi grew older, he developed a longing for the land of Israel and wrote a number of beautiful poems called "Songs of Zion." One of them, the "Ode to Zion," is chanted by Jews throughout the world on the Ninth of Av, the day of fasting and mourning for the destruction of the Temple.

Jerusalem and Zion were like a holy flame that throbbed inside Judah Halevi. To him Zion was the city where the Shechinah—God's Holy Presence—dwelled on earth.

Like most of the Spanish-Jewish poets, Judah was interested in philosophy. His most important philosophical work was the *Kuzari* ("The Khazar"). Some years earlier King Bulan, the ruler of the Khazars, a people living near the Caspian Sea in what is now Russia, had written to Chasdi Ibn Shaprut, a high-ranking Spanish-Jewish official, telling how his people had converted to Judaism. This letter gave Judah Halevi the idea for a dialogue in which a rabbi explains Judaism to the Khazar monarch. At the end of the book, the rabbi bids farewell to the king and sets out on a journey to Palestine.

In his old age Judah Halevi also set out to see the land of Israel. His friends and relatives tried to stop him, for the journey was long and dangerous. But the poet would not change his mind. He crossed the Mediterranean Sea and traveled through North Africa, visiting the Jewish communities along the way. In Cairo, Egypt, many urged him to give up the idea of continuing to Israel, but the old man was determined to see his dream fulfilled.

Judah Halevi never returned from his journey. When he reached the gates of Jerusalem, he fell upon his knees and kissed the holy ground. As he knelt there he was trampled to death by the horse of an Arab rider. So the poet Judah Halevi died—standing at last on the soil of the beloved land of Israel. Judah Halevi was the prophet of his generation, and a guide and influence for centuries to come.

MATCH THE COLUMNS

1. Cordova		Khazar
2. Southern Spain		Chasdai Ibn Shaprut
3. Judah Halevi		Andalusia
4. "Ode to Zion"		Capital of caliphate
5. *Kuzari*		Jewish poet

FILL IN THE BLANKS

1. The _____ rulers wanted all of their subjects to participate in the life of the new commonwealth.

2. Judah developed a love for the land of _____ and wrote beautiful poems called _____ .

3. Halevi's most important work was the _____.

4. The *Kuzari* is based on the letter from _____ to _____ .

5. In the *Kuzari,* the _____ is Halevi's spokesman and appears before the monarch.

Bulan, Songs of Zion, Moslem, rabbi, Israel, Kuzari, Khazar, Chasdai Ibn Shaprut

ANSWER THE QUESTIONS

1. Why did Judah Halevi decide to go to Palestine?
2. How did the Moorish conquerors treat their new subjects?
3. Why was the period of the Andalusian caliphate called the Golden Age of Spanish Jewry?
4. Who helped familiarize the Jews of Spain with the Talmud?
5. Whom did Judah credit for his medical skills?

JUDAH HALEVI AND YOU

In this poem, Judah Halevi explains his love for the Sabbath.

To love you I drink my cup,
Shalom to you, shalom, O seventh day.
The first six days are like your slaves;
I work restlessly through them,
But they seem like only a few days because
of my love for you, O wonderful day.

1. From what kind of cup is Judah drinking?
2. What does he means when he describes the first six days of the week as slavery?
3. Can a job be a kind of slavery?
4. What makes the six days of slavery worthwhile, besides payday?
5. How is Shabbat freedom from slavery?
6. How can you, like Judah Halevi, make Shabbat a wonderful day for you and your family?

The *Kuzari*

THE *KUZARI* DESCRIBES THE CONVERSION to Judaism in the year 740 of the Khazars, a warlike people located near the Caspian Sea, in what is now Russia. The structure of the *Kuzari* is a conversation in which a Christian, a Moslem, and a Jew appear before Bulan, king of the Khazars, to describe their respective religions.

The rabbi, Halevi's spokesman, describes Judaism's prayers, history, and views on God. He states that Judaism is based on a historic appearance of God that 600,000 Israelites, who had been freed from slavery, saw, felt, and experienced at Mount Sinai. The Jews were not persuaded to believe in God by debates or logic but experienced God's presence by direct personal contact.

At the end of the debate, King Bulan is convinced and converts his entire kingdom to Judaism.

THE GOLDEN AGE OF SPANISH JEWRY lasted for three centuries, starting around the year 900. The situation began to change when the Almohades, a fanatical Moslem sect from North Africa, invaded Andalusia. With the fall of Cordova in 1149, the Almohades became the new rulers of Moslem Spain.

Unlike the earlier Moslem rulers, the Almohades sought to convert everyone to Islam. They persecuted Jews and Christians alike, forcing them to become Moslems or leave the land.

Many Spanish Jews set out for North Africa. Among them was Moses Maimonides. When he was 13 years old, his family fled to North Africa to escape persecution. There, as in Spain, Moses studied with his father, who was a judge to the Jewish community. Several years later the family moved to Jerusalem. Because of the crusaders in Palestine, the family was once again forced to flee. This time they went to Egypt.

Moses Maimonides is often called Rambam in Hebrew, an acronym for *Rabbenu Mosheh ben Maimon*. Maimonides was well versed in Hebrew, the Bible, the Talmud, and other Jewish writings. He also studied mathematics and astronomy, Arabic literature and Greek philosophy. Moses even managed to study medicine and became a skilled physician.

The reason we know so much about Maimonides and his family is the genizah in Fostat, a town in Egypt. Every ancient synagogue had a storeroom called a genizah. In it were placed old prayerbooks and religious objects that could not be destroyed because they contained God's name. Often the genizah was also the storehouse for business documents and personal correspondence.

Around the beginning of the 20th century, Professor Solomon Schechter began to catalogue and translate the 200,000 Hebrew and Arabic documents in the genizah of the Ezra Synagogue in Fostat. This was the very synagogue where Maimonides had taught and prayed.

The treasure trove included hundreds of business letters from Moses Maimonides' younger brother David. The letters give many details about his travels and business activities, as well as about the family.

The genizah documents tell us much about Maimonides' personal life. In one letter he writes, "The ordinary people find it difficult to visit me in Fostat, so I am forced to greet them in Cairo. When I get home I am too tired to study."

Maimonides: 1135–1204

EVEN AS A YOUNG MAN, Maimonides wrote brilliant books and essays. When the Jews of Morocco were hard-pressed by the Almohades to become Moslems, they asked Maimonides what they should do. He advised them to leave the place of forced conversion; "Whoever remains in such a place," he said, "desecrates the Divine Name and is nearly as a bad as a willful sinner."

After much wandering, Maimonides and his family went to Egypt. He set up a medical practice in the city of Fostat, near Cairo. His fame spread, and before long he became the personal physician of Sultan Saladin and the royal family. Rich and poor, Jews and Moslems alike, patients of every background consulted him, and the great physician found time to see them all. The wealthy paid for his services, but the poor were treated free of charge.

At the request of the *nagid*, the leader of the Jewish community, Maimonides also took on the responsibility of providing religious guidance to the Jews of Egypt. He became a greatly beloved teacher. After Sabbath

services each week, he gave public lectures on Talmud and Torah.

Despite his many duties, Maimonides managed to write the most important code of Jewish law since the completion of the Talmud. This great halachic code is called the *Mishneh Torah* ("Repetition of the Torah") or *Yad HaChazakah* ("The Strong Hand").

The *Mishneh Torah* codifies all the laws in the Mishnah and the Talmud, together with the commentaries of the gaonim and the scholars in the generations following them.

Maimonides' best-known philosophical work is the *Moreh Nevukhim* ("Guide for the Perplexed"), written in Arabic. In it he clearly explains the principles and ideas of Judaism.

When Maimonides died in Fostat in 1204, he was mourned throughout the Jewish world. People compared him to the great leader who had led the Israelites out of Egypt in ancient times, saying, "From Moses to Moses, there was none like Moses."

MATCH THE COLUMNS

1. Maimonides   Leader of Egyptian Jews
2. *Nagid*   Storeroom
3. *Moreh Nevukhim*   900–1200 C.E.
4. *Mishneh Torah*   Rambam
5. Golden Age   Laws of Mishnah and Torah
6. Genizah   "Guide for the Perplexed"

FILL IN THE BLANKS

1. _____ set up his medical practice in the town of _____.

2. The _____ invaded Spain and conquered _____.

3. The *Mishneh Torah* codifies all the laws of the _____ and the _____.

4. "From _____ to Moses, there was none like Moses."

5. The _____ of _____ lasted for 300 years.

Golden Age, Mishnah, Maimonides, Almohades, Moses, Talmud, Fostat, Moslim Spain, Spain

ANSWER THE QUESTIONS

1. Who brought an end to the Golden Age of Spain?
2. Why did Jews in Fostat build a genizah?
3. How did Maimonides get the name Rambam?
4. What did Maimonides advise the Jews of Morocco to do in order to avoid conversion?

MAIMONIDES AND YOU

Rambam, in his *Mishneh Torah,* described the eight approaches to giving charity. All of them are commendable, because giving charity is always a mitzvah, but the approaches are ranked in an order of precedence. The first on the list is the lowest, the eighth and last is the highest and most noble. It has this status because it enables the recipient to become self-supporting and no longer dependent on charity.

1. *The donor gives unwillingly.*
2. *The donor gives cheerfully, but not enough.*
3. *The donor gives enough, but not until asked.*
4. *The donor gives before being asked, but directly to the poor person.*
5. *The recipient knows who the donor is, but the donor does not know the identity of the recipient.*
6. *The giver knows who the recipient is, but the recipient does not know the donor's identity.*
7. *The donor does not know who the recipient is, and the recipient does not know who the donor is.*
8. *Instead of simply giving charity, the donor makes the poor person self-sufficient by lending him the money to start a business, entering into a partnership with him, or providing training in a trade or craft.*

1. What is the lowest from of giving charity?
2. What is the highest form of charity?
3. Why did Maimonides think that #8 was the highest form of tzedakah?
4. Do you agree?
5. Look at #5 and #6; why is #6 a greater mitzvah than #5?
6. What makes #7 greater than #5 and #6?
7. Do you agree with the order of this tzedakah ladder?
8. Would you rearrange it? How?
9. What is wrong with giving tzedakah face-to-face to a poor person?
10. Which degree of charity would you choose?
11. How would you feel giving directly to the poor? How would the poor person feel knowing that you have given him charity?

World History: 12th–13th century

AS SPAIN'S CHRISTIANS gradually began reconquering the country, more and more Jews came under their rule. The Christians made an all-out effort to convert them. Children were kidnapped and baptized. Enraged mobs rampaged through Jewish neighborhoods, offering the residents a choice between the church and the cross or death and the Torah. In the end, about a third of Spain's Jews chose Christianity just to save their lives. Reduced taxes and economic opportunity created a ideal environment for conversion.

The forced converts were known as Marranos, and also as New Christians, in contrast to Old Christians who had been born into the Christian faith. By forcing the Marranos to convert, the Old Christians had unwittingly opened up areas of activity for them from which they had been excluded as Jews.

Because they proved to be so successful in these areas, the Marranos soon aroused much Old Christian resentment. Before long Marranos were advancing to positions of great political and financial influence. The Old Christians did not like this; their envy aroused, they began seeking a way to eliminate their Marrano competitors.

The weapon they adopted was the Inquisition. During the 12th century, the leaders of the Catholic Church had become concerned about the spread of heresy—beliefs and practices not in strict accord with Catholic teachings. In 1233, Pope Gregory IV set up a special commission called the Inquisition to stamp our heresy by identifying and punishing heretics.

The Inquisition was originally established to deal with Christian heretics, but now it turned its attention to the Jews of Spain. Some of them had returned to Judaism after their forced conversions to Christianity; many others pretended outwardly to be Christians, but continued to observe Judaism secretly.

Jews of both types were technically regarded as heretics and therefore came under the Inquisition's jurisdiction. Marranos who were observed changing bedsheets on Friday or leaving a candle burning were arrested. Those whom the Inquisition could not persuade to abandon Judaism were burned at the stake in a public ceremony known as an auto-da-fé. In the years that followed, thousands of Marranos were tortured and burned to death.

In an effort to persuade Spain's Jews and Marranos that Christianity was the only true religion, a convert appropriately named Pablo Christiani persuaded the king of Aragon to force Moses ben Nachman, Spanish Jewry's foremost scholar, to debate him publicly on the belief in Jesus.

Rabbi Moses ben Nachman: 1194–1270

The rabbi chosen to defend Judaism in the debate before the royal court and high-ranking church dignitaries was Moses ben Nachman, also known as Nachmanides and as Ramban (from *Rabbi Mosheh ben Nachman*).

Nachmanides was Spanish Jewry's most important scholar and rabbinic leader. He earned his living as a doctor and also served as rabbi of the town of Gerona.

Nachmanides proudly stood before the court and the king, facing the fanatical Pablo and the other church officials. In the debate Pablo tried to prove that Jesus was the Messiah, quoting isolated talmudic statements to support his claim. Nachmanides easily contradicted him. The statements quoted by Pablo, he explained, were legends and tales that had no historical bearing on what Jews believed. The important part of the Talmud was its legal portion, the halachah, and this contained nothing whatsoever to support Pablo's arguments.

The wisdom of the aged Nachmanides impressed the king, who ended the debate without declaring Pablo the victor. On parting with Nachmanides, the king gave him a generous gift.

Not long afterwards Nachmanides published a transcript of the debate. Although the debate would have been publicized if the

Christian spokesman had won, church officials were not eager to have Nachmanides' spirited defense of Judaism circulated.

When Pablo heard what Nachmanides had done, he reported it to the king. Once again Nachmanides was summoned to appear before the king. At the insistence of church officials he was sentenced to two years in exile.

Nachmanides left Spain and went to Palestine. The aged scholar devoted the last years of his life to the Jews of Palestine. He built a synagogue in Jerusalem and opened a school. Scholars and students gathered around him. Before his death Nachmanides saw the results of his work. The religious life of the Jews the land of Israel had been enriched and revitalized through his efforts.

Today in Jerusalem there is a synagogue in the Old City called the Ramban Synagogue. It is believed to have originally been situated on Mount Zion. However, it was moved to its present site around 1400. A letter written by Nachmanides about the miserable state of the Jewish community is displayed there.

In the 16th century the Turkish government prohibited Jews from praying in the Ramban Synagogue and it became a workshop. During the British Mandate it was converted into a store. When the Israelis captured the Old City during the Six-Day War in 1967 it was rebuilt, and it is now used as a synagogue again.

MATCH THE COLUMNS

1. New Christians	Messiah
2. Pablo Christiani	Nachmanides
3. Moses ben Nachman	Marranos
4. Inquisition	Convert
5. Jesus	Christian heretics

FILL IN THE BLANKS

1. _____ was Spanish Jewry's most important rabbinic leader.

2. Nachmanides went to _____ and was distressed by the state of the _____ living there.

3. Nachmanides built a _____ and opened a school in Jerusalem.

4. The _____ was set up to punish people who were spreading heresies.

5. The _____ aroused the envy of the old _____.

Christians, synagogue, Jews, Marranos, Inquisition, Nachmanides, Palestine

ANSWER THE QUESTIONS

1. Why did the Jewish community choose Moses ben Nachman to debate Pablo Christiani?
2. Who was Pablo Christiani?
3. Why was the Catholic Church concerned about the spread of heresy?
4. How did the clergy deal with heretics?
5. Why did the Old Christians resent the Marranos?
6. Why was Nachmanides distressed about the state of the Jews in Palestine?
7. How did Nachmanides spend his last years in Palestine?

RABBI MOSES BEN NACHMAN AND YOU

Rabbi Moses ben Nachman was chosen to defend the Jews of Spain in a debate against Pablo Christiani. During the debate, he had to be very careful not to insult Christianity and to control his temper.

After the debate, he wrote a letter to his son in which he said:

Think before you speak.

1. Was this advice important for Rabbi Moses ben Nachman during the debate? Why?
2. Was it dangerous for him to say exactly what was on his mind?
3. Is this advice important for everyone?
4. Can thinking save you from getting into trouble?
5. How can you make sure to think before speaking?

Another one of Rabbi Moses ben Nachman's sayings was:

When you pray, remove from your heart all worldly concerns.

Concentration during prayer is called Kavanah.

If you have true Kavanah your mind is free from other thoughts during prayer, and you are aware that you are standing before the Holy One—God.

When you are in a state of Kavanah you stop thinking about making plans, arranging a meeting, practicing tennis, doing homework, singing, making music, taking trips, playing with friends. You stop worrying. You do not have to do anything or go anywhere. Everything is nothing. You are standing before your Creator.

How do you know when you have achieved Kavanah? When you feel feally good after praying. When you surprise yourself and say, "Wow, I enjoyed temple services." When you leave the synagogue and sing the tunes out loud. When you do a mitzvah and hadn't planned to do it.

THE MARRANOS were constantly watched by spies and informers. Anyone suspected of practicing Judaism was arrested by the Inquisition. The property of those arrested was confiscated. Most of them were tortured. Many were burned at the stake in a ceremony called the auto-da-fé.

Finding Marranos was a huge money-making project. Very often people were arrested and tortured simply because they were well-to-do. Their confiscated property was divided between the church and the crown. Sometimes people were accused of being secret Jews and arrested simply because someone had a grudge against them.

The Inquisition, led by Tomás de Torquemada, warned Queen Isabella and King Ferdinand that the presence of Jews in Spain was bad for the church and would weaken the country. If the Jews were forced to leave Spain, he said, it would be much easier to control the Marranos.

The king and queen agreed, but put off doing anything because the Jews were still needed for their important political and economic contribution to Spain's national power. Spain was at war with Granada, the last Moslem outpost in Spanish territory, and it would have weakened the war effort if the many thousands of Jewish army officers, map makers, doctors, ammunition makers, and businessmen were driven out of the country.

However, Granada surrendered on January 2, 1492. King Ferdinand and Queen Isabella triumphantly entered the city. Now in control of all of Spain, they gave in and agreed to banish the Jews.

The date of the expulsion, on the Hebrew calendar, was the ninth day of the month of Av in the year 1492. This was the very same day on which the First Temple had been destroyed by the Babylonians in 586 B.C.E. and the Second Temple had been destroyed by the Romans in 70 C.E.

Everything had to be left behind. Jews who had property traded it for sturdy traveling clothes. Precious jewels were exchanged for food for the long perilous journey. Like ants feasting on a dead body, the priests surrounded the exiles and even invaded the synagogues. They urged the hapless victims to convert and save their lives and their property. A few consented, but the majority chose to go into exile.

On the second day of August in 1492, 300,000 Jews left Spain. Among them was Don Isaac Abravanel, one of Spain's most important officials.

Don Isaac Abravanel: 1437–1508

DON ISAAC ABRAVANEL WAS BORN IN PORTUGAL in 1437, to a family that was socially and politically prominent. His education included Hebrew, Talmud, mathematics, science, Greek literature, and the writings of Christian and Moslem scholars.

Isaac's father, Judah, was the royal treasurer of Portugal. His parents' home was a meeting place for Jewish, Christian, and Moslem scholars, politicians, and financiers. From them Isaac learned the arts of diplomacy and high finance.

King Alfonso V of Portugal, under whom Jews enjoyed freedom and prosperity, appointed Isaac as his treasurer when his father died. Isaac helped his people whenever he could. When Jewish captives in Morocco were being sold as slaves, he personally intervened and managed to ransom and free all of them.

After Alfonso's death in 1482, Isaac Abravanel's enemies accused him of plotting against the crown and he was forced to flee to Spain.

After his escape Abravanel settled in the city of Toledo. Now, at the age of 40, he devoted himself to his first love, writing a commentary on the Bible. This work was interrupted when Isaac was summoned to appear at the court of King Ferdinand and Queen Isabella.

At that moment in history, Spain was beset by many political, economic, and military problems. The rulers needed a miracle worker who could pull the country out of its troubles. In a short time Abravanel managed to replenish the Spanish treasury, mobilize the country's resources, and resupply the army with food and arms.

When Ferdinand and Isabella issued the order expelling the Jews from Spain, Abravanel tried to get them to change their minds. He offered an enormous sum if the expulsion order was cancelled.

King Ferdinand, who took more interest in his treasury than in the Catholic faith, wanted to accept the bribe and rescind the order. Then the fanatical grand inquisitor Torquemada shouted, "Judas Iscariot sold Christ for 30 pieces of silver, now your highnesses are about to sell him for 300,000 ducats. Here he is, take him and sell him!"

Although Abravanel's plea was unsuccessful, he could have stayed in Spain if he wished, because Ferdinand and Isabella offered to exempt him from the expulsion order. Instead he cast his lot with his friends and brethren, the Jewish people. Like Moses leading the children of Israel out of Egypt, he led the exodus from Spain.

After much wandering, Abravanel found a refuge in a town near Naples, Italy. Notwithstanding his advanced years, Don Isaac managed to complete his commentary on most of the Bible. His discussions of the kings of Judah and Israel are extremely illuminating, because he intimately knew the ways of kings, governments, and their intrigues.

Abravanel died in 1508, at a ripe old age, and was buried in Padua, Italy. In 1904, the Jews of Padua erected a monument in the cemetery in memory of Don Isaac Abravanel.

MATCH THE COLUMNS

1. Inquisition   Expulsion
2. King Ferdinand   Abravanel's burial place
3. Ninth of Av, 1492   Jewish author
4. Abravanel   Torquemada
5. Padua   Queen Isabella

FILL IN THE BLANKS

1. The _____ was led by the Grand Inquisitor _____ .

2. Jews played an important role in the political and economic life of _____ .

3. Like Moses leading the Israelites out of Egypt, _____ led the _____ out of Spain.

4. King _____ took more interest in the treasury than in his _____ faith.

5. Don Isaac Abravanel wrote a commentary on the _____ .

Catholic, Torah, Inquisition, Don Isaac, Spain, Ferdinand, Torquemada, expulsion, Jews

ANSWER THE QUESTIONS

1. Who was Torquemada?
2. Why did he want to drive the Jews out of Spain?
3. Why was Abravanel forced to escape to Portugal?
4. Why did King Ferdinand and Queen Isabella invite Abravanel to settle in Spain?
5. What trick did Torquemada use to force the king and queen to expel the Jews?
6. How did Abravanel's experience with royalty and governments help him write his commentary on the Bible?

DON ISAAC ABRAVANEL AND YOU

Isaac Abravanel was raised in a wealthy home with lots of servants. He thought of money as a means of doing good deeds for his people. This was Isaac Abravanel's credo:

God does not want us to keep away from pleasures and the good things on earth. The Torah tells us to keep the middle way. One should not feel that it is wrong to have wealth, if it is honestly gained, and does not interfere with study and good deeds.

1.   What did Isaac Abravanel think about wealth?
2.   Why was Abravanel comfortable with money and riches?
3.   Can money corrupt a person? How?
4.   Can money be used for special purposes?

The Torah tells us that a person should donate 10% of his or her yearly income to charity. This kind of personal tax is caller *Ma'aser*. The word *ma'aser* comes from the Hebrew word *eser,* meaning "ten." In English, it is called a tithe. Today, there are many Jews who practice tithing.

1.   What do you think about making a commitment to tithe a person's income?
2.   Do you know anyone who is committed to tithing?
3.   What do you think about tithing your allowance? To whom or to what project would you commit your tithe?

World History: 13th–16th century

STARTING IN THE 13TH CENTURY, the Ottoman Turks expanded militarily and conquered many territories. Hordes of galloping Turkish cavalrymen carved out a large state in Asia Minor and parts of Europe. Their unstoppable advance brought an end to the decadent, thousand-year-old Byzantine Empire. On May 13, 1453 the armies of Sultan Mahomet II completed the Turkish victory by capturing the Byzantine capital of Constantinople, which was renamed Istanbul.

Proud of his victory, the Sultan realized that his warriors knew how to fight a war, but lacked the skills and education to run a great empire. Mahomet did not trust the political reliability of the Greek and Armenian middle class in the newly conquered lands. He realized that the Jews expelled from Spain were just what was needed for the economic and cultural development of his empire.

Mahomet II invited the Jewish exiles to settle in Turkey, guaranteeing them protection and religious freedom. In a short time, a tremendous number accepted his invitation and began flooding into the Ottoman domains. The Sultan welcomed the newcomers with open arms. One Turkish official exclaimed, "How can you consider King Ferdinand a wise ruler when he has impoverished his own land and enriched ours?"

The influx of highly educated, enterprising Sephardic Jews brought rich seeds of culture, commerce, and industry to the Ottoman world. Among the refugees were scientists who familiarized the Turks with the latest inventions in military science and established factories to manufacture gunpowder and cannons.

One of the wanderers who found a home in the Turkish Empire was a young scholar named Joseph ben Ephraim Karo.

Joseph Karo: 1488–1575

BORN IN SPAIN in 1488, Joseph Karo lived through the great expulsion as a four-year-old. After long wanderings his family settled in Turkey.

Even as a child Karo was recognized as a genius, and his fame spread rapidly. While still a young man he was appointed rabbi of Nicopolis, in what is now Bulgaria. Eventually he settled in Safed, Israel, where he became the head of an academy of Jewish learning.

In 1522 Joseph Karo began writing the *Bet Yosef* ("House of Joseph"). This monumental four-volume work was an encyclopedic code of talmudic law. Karo spent more than 20 years on it.

After finishing the *Bet Yosef,* Rabbi Joseph Karo spent another 10 years preparing a shorter code, the *Shulchan Aruch* ("Prepared Table"). This was intended as a handy reference for those seeking detailed halachic guidance on Jewish practices and customs. The *Shulchan Aruch* quickly became popular because it consisted of short, simple statements that explained what to do in any given situation without complicated elaborations or digressions.

Initially the *Shulchan Aruch* met with opposition from Ashkenazic scholars because it was based on halachic decisions by Sephardic rabbis and sometimes disregarded French and German traditions. This problem was overcome by Rabbi Moses Isserles (1525–1572), also known as Rema, of Cracow, Poland. Rema added explanations of Ashkenazic practice to Rabbi Karo's text, making it suitable for use by all Jews everywhere.

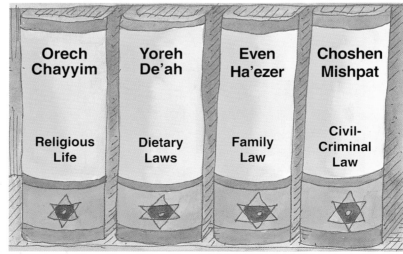

Orech Chayyim — Religious Life

Yoreh De'ah — Dietary Laws

Even Ha'ezer — Family Law

Choshen Mishpat — Civil-Criminal Law

The *Bet Yosef* was Rabbi Joseph Karo's beloved child, and the *Shulchan Aruch* was secondary, a stepchild. Nevertheless, it was the *Shulchan Aruch* that came to play a most important role in Judaism. It became a cornerstone of rabbinic Judaism.

Rabbi Karo was, in a way, a two-sided personality. Although he had a methodical, down-to-earth, encyclopedic mind, he was, at the same time, a believer in the mystical teachings of the Kabbalah. In fact he was a follower of Solomon Molcho, a Marrano mystic whose Christian name was Diego Pires.

Joseph Karo was hypnotized by Molcho's fiery speeches and prophetic visions, and the two men became fast friends. Solomon Molcho's influence on Karo was so great that he began seeing visions of a higher being called a Maggid who revealed heavenly secrets to him. He claimed that the Maggid visited him every Shabbat and on holidays.

Rabbi Joseph Karo was regarded as Safed's leading halachic scholar, and his yeshiva had more than 200 students. In addition to his duties he also found time to write hundreds of responsa to halachic inquiries.

Joseph Karo died in Safed at the age of 87. His name has been immortalized by his most famous book, the *Shulchan Aruch*. It is the authoritative book of Jewish law for Orthodox Jewry throughout the world.

MATCH THE COLUMNS

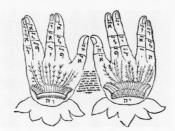

1. Ottoman   Marrano
2. *Shulchan Aruch*   Turkish
3. Rabbi Moshe Isserles   Higher being
4. Maggid   "Prepared Table"
5. *Bet Yosef*   Ashkenazi
6. Solomon Molcho   "House of Joseph"

FILL IN THE BLANKS

1. The *Shulchan Aruch* is a short version of the _____.

2. Rabbi _____ added Ashkenazic explanations to the *Shulchan Aruch*.

3. _____ became a follower of the _____ Solomon Molcho.

4. Joseph Karo believed that a higher heavenly being called _____ visited him on Shabbat and on Jewish holidays.

5. The Ottomans realized that the _____ were an ideal middle class for the development of their empire.

**Joseph Karo, Marrano, Maggid, Bet Yosef,
Moses Isserles, Jews**

ANSWER THE QUESTIONS

1. Why did the Ottoman Turks welcome the Jews?
2. Why did Joseph Karo decide to write the *Bet Yosef*?
3. What was the *Shulchan Aruch*?
4. Why was it called the *Shulchan Aruch*?
5. What was the difference between the *Shulchan Aruch* and the *Bet Yosef*?
6. Why did the Ashkenazim at first not accept the *Shulchan Aruch*?
7. Who was the Maggid, and whom did he visit?

JOSEPH KARO AND YOU

In one of his books, Joseph Karo gives this advice:

If you want to take revenge on your enemy, become a fine and good person, whom everyone admires and speaks well of. In this way your enemy will be annoyed when he hears words of praise spoken about you. But if you want to make your enemy happy, then do wrong things and he will rejoice over your disgrace and shame.

1. How can your being a fine person anger an enemy?
2. Why would words of praise from a third person anger a competitor?
3. Why would a competitor love to hear bad things about his so-called enemy?
4. What does it mean to be a "good kid"? Can a kid like you have an enemy?
5. Is someone who competes against you in sports or in school an enemy or an opponent?
6. What's the difference between an enemy and an opponent?
7. Is someone who spreads lies about you, or is jealous of your accomplishments, an enemy or a competitor?
8. Can you avenge yourself by keeping quiet and just continuing to excel at school or in sports?
9. Do you think your competitor would be annoyed if you ignored him or her and continued to do well?
10. How can you make your detractors happy?
11. What do you think of Joseph Karo's statement? What does it teach you?

World History: 14th–16th century

THE BODY OF MYSTICAL KNOWLEDGE comprising the Kabbalah developed over hundreds of years. In the 13th century most of these teachings were compiled in a book called the Zohar by Moses de Leon of Castile, Spain. Written in Aramaic and organized as a commentary on the Torah, it expounded sacred mysteries hidden from ordinary readers of the Bible.

According to Moses de Leon, the Zohar dated back to the 2nd century C.E. and had been written by Simeon bar Yochai, a colleague of Rabbi Akiba. Moses claimed to have found it in a cave in which Simeon bar Yochai and his son Eliezer had hidden for 13 years during the Roman persecution in the time of Hadrian. Throughout this period, the Talmud records, Simeon and his son ate the fruit of a carob tree and spent their time studying the mysteries of the Torah.

The Zohar fascinated Jewish scholars, and in the next few centuries interest in Kabbalah spread from Spain to other countries. The kabbalists maintained that every aspect of the Torah—even including the shapes of the letters and variations in spelling that sometimes look like errors—had a secret meaning that could be

uncovered through intensive study. All these hidden meanings were set forth in the Zohar, for those who knew how to find them.

The Zohar also teaches that every act of every human being has an effect on the world above. When we perform good deeds, we crown the day with goodness, and it becomes our protection in the world to come. But if we perform a cruel deed, it has a negative effect on the day and will destroy us in the world to come. Thus good and bad deeds can build or destroy the balance of the earth.

Some of the formulas and symbols developed by the mystics are utilized in the prayerbook. The blowing of the shofar, for instance, is introduced with a kabbalistic prayer. The prayer before reading the Torah is also introduced with a passage from the Zohar, Berich Shemei.

The expulsion from Spain in 1492 helped to increase interest in mystical lore. Jews of Spanish origin became the leaders in the study of the Kabbalah. It attracted them because they were seeking an explanation for the misfortunes they had undergone.

Safed, in Israel, became the center of the kabbalistic movement. It was an ideal place for this purpose. The beauty of the surrounding hills and the mysterious echoes which reverberated through the valleys inspired the saintliness of the Safed kabbalists. Isaac Luria was one of the most important kabbalists who was attracted to Safed and settled there.

Rabbi Isaac Luria: 1534–1572

THE GREATEST TEACHER OF KABBALAH in Safed was the brilliant young Rabbi Isaac Luria. Born in Jerusalem, he lost his father when he was a child, but was brought to Cairo, where he was educated under the care of his uncle. Luria made rapid progress in his rabbinic studies and became acquainted with the Kabbalah, to which he vigorously applied himself.

When Rabbi Isaac Luria settled in Safed, he found many enthusiastic students there. By devoting themselves to the joys of mysticism and prayer, they hoped to hasten the coming of the Messiah and the time of eternal peace.

Rabbi Luria's saintly way of life, personality, and approach to kabbalistic study soon won him the affection and loyalty of Safed's mystical community. After he died at the young age of 38, they preserved his teachings and transmitted them to later generations.

Luria's students referred to him as the Ari, an acronym for *Adoneinu Rabbi Yitzchak* ("Our master, Rabbi Isaac"). *Ari* is the Hebrew word meaning "lion." The disciples of Rabbi Isaac thought him as courageous, strong, and mighty as a lion, the ancient symbol of the tribe of Judah.

Many talmudic scholars regarded the kabbalists as misguided and dangerous. They said that the kabbalists did not show much interest in Jewish law and halachic issues. Their way of life differed from the disciplined life of the scholars. As time went on, the conflict between these two approaches to Judaism became more intense. But in Safed, in the days of Rabbi Isaac Luria, they existed peacefully, side-by-side.

After Isaac Luria's death during a plague in 1572, his followers built a synagogue where they would gather to welcome the Sabbath. This synagogue was destroyed in an earthquake in 1852. The rebuilt synagogue has a shrapnel hole from an Arab attack during Israel's War of Independence in 1948.

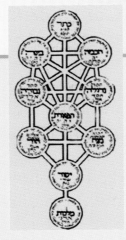

MATCH THE COLUMNS

1. Zohar   Ari
2. Kabbalah   Mystical studies
3. Isaac Luria   Palestinian city
4. Safed   Moses de Leon

FILL IN THE BLANKS

1. According to _____, the Zohar was written by _____.

2. The hidden meanings of the Torah are found in the _____.

3. The Zohar is written in _____.

4. _____ was an ideal city for the study of _____.

Simeon bar Yochai, Aramaic, Safed, Moses de Leon, Zohar, Kabbalah

ANSWER THE QUESTIONS

1. Why did the expulsion from Spain increase interest in the Kabbalah?
2. Why was Safed an ideal city for kabbalists?
3. How did the kabbalists hope to speed up the coming of the Messiah?
4. Why did the students call Luria "Ari"?
5. Why did some scholars regard the kabbalists as dangerous?

ISAAC LURIA AND YOU

During the Yom Kippur service, we recite a confessional prayer called Al Chet. This prayer is written in the plural form; in it we ask God to forgive us for the sins we have committed.

Rabbi Isaac Luria asked a question and also answered it:

Question: **Why is the Al Chet written in the plural form?**
Answer: **Because all of Israel is one body, and every Jew is a member of that body. Therefore it follows that all Jews are responsible for each other.**

1. Why did Luria compare the Jewish people to a body?
2. Who are its arms and legs?
3. Who are its brains?
4. What does it mean for a Jew to be responsible for a fellow Jew?
5. Does it means that you have to help your fellow Jew?
6. How can you help a fellow Jew who is in Russia, France, or the North Pole?
7. Are you obliged to help your classmates?
8. Are there ways you can be helpful to fellow Jews?
9. Should you help only Jews, or other people too?
10. Suppose two organizations asked you for help, one Jewish and one non-Jewish. Which would you help first?

World History: 18th–19th century

TOWARD THE END OF THE MIDDLE AGES, large numbers of Jews from Germany settled in Poland, which at that time included much of Lithuania and Ukraine. They came at the invitation of the Polish kings, who needed them because of their advanced commercial and technical skills. In the years that followed Polish Jewry prospered. Governed by a body of rabbis known as the Council of Four Lands, Polish Jews were able to live under their own laws and spoke their own language, Yiddish.

There was always a certain amount of anti-Jewish hostility among Poland's peasants and Christian clergy, but by and large Polish Jewry prospered. The situation changed radically after 1648, when the Cossacks of Ukraine rose up in revolt under the leadership of Bogdan Chmielnicki.

The Cossacks killed thousands of Jews in brutal pogroms. Jewish communities were destroyed, and Jewish property was looted.

In the aftermath of the revolt, conditions for the Jews steadily deteriorated. The Council of Four Lands was abolished by the government. Communities that had been rebuilt after the Chmielnicki pogroms went into a decline. Many communities were so poor they could not even maintain their school systems.

The Polish government was also gravely weakened. Three times the land was invaded and partitioned by its more powerful neighbors. By 1796, nothing remained and Poland lost its independence. Depending upon where they lived, the Jews of Poland now became subjects of either Russia, Prussia, or Austria.

The ruler of Russia in 1796 was Catherine the Great. She regarded herself as a liberal empress, but her subjects lived under primitive conditions. The partitions of Poland brought Catherine the lion's share of Polish Jewry. In order to prevent this mass of Jews from expanding into other parts of her empire, she restricted their right of residence to the areas taken from Poland in which they were already living.

This area was known as the Pale of Settlement. It included eastern Poland, Ukraine, and Lithuania. In addition to its Jewish residents, it had a much larger population of Christians who hated their Jewish neighbors.

It was here, in the little towns and villages of the Pale, in a few crowded cities and lonely inns along the highway, that most of Europe's Jews were to live for the next 200 years. The Russian government imposed many harsh restrictions upon them. They had to pay high taxes and could not move or travel without permission; they could not attend Russian schools or academies of higher learning and were barred from many other public institutions.

Nonetheless, Jewish life in the Pale was active and full. While all but a few Russian nobles were illiterate, even the humblest Jewish family sent its son to the one-room cheder to learn to read and write and engage in studying the Torah. The very restrictions that had been imposed upon them served to knit the Jews of the Pale to a way of life based on brotherhood, neighborliness, and genuine concern for one another.

This period was to produce two great religious leaders, each quite different from the other and each concerned with a different way of life. One was Israel ben Eliezer, known as the Baal Shem Tov; the other was Elijah ben Solomon, the Gaon of Vilna.

ישְׂרָאֵל בֶּן אֱלִיעֶזֶר בַּעַל שֵׁם טוֹב (בֶּעֶשׁ״ט)
Israel ben Eliezer: 1698–1760

ISRAEL BEN ELIEZER WAS BORN IN A SMALL TOWN in Ukraine about 1698. When still a small child he lost both his parents and was cared for by the community. After graduating from the cheder he became the assistant to the teacher.

Israel liked children, and they, in turn, loved to listen to his stories. He took great delight in roaming the woods around the town and often would take his pupils with him. There, amidst the wonders of nature, teacher and pupils would chant the psalms and the melodies of the prayers.

Israel married a young woman called Hannah, and the two moved to a village in the Carpathian Mountains, where Israel earned his living as a lime digger. He enjoyed his work, for while it brought him very little money, it left him time to study and to meditate on God and life.

For seven years Israel and Hannah lived in solitude in the mountains. All around him Israel could behold the beauty God had created. The humble lime digger was convinced that the holiness, or Shechinah, of God dwelt within every living thing. Everyone, scholar and simple laborer alike, could reach spiritual heights by prayer and by being kind and loving to all creatures.

The "worship of the heart" through joy and ecstasy, Israel taught, was of greater importance than dry, routine, ritual observance. Some of his famous stories illustrate this point.

In one story, a shepherd boy who does not know how to read

the Siddur prays, one solemn Yom Kippur, by blowing his whistle. It is the only way he has to express his intense love for God. Because it is sincere and genuine, it is a legitimate way for him to pray.

In another story, a lad who only knows the letters of the Hebrew alphabet recites them as his prayer, feeling sure that God will put them together in the right combinations.

Israel ben Eliezer's teachings appealed to many people, especially those who were poor and uneducated. He wrote no books; his wisdom was spread by word of mouth among rabbis and among the tradesmen, artisans, and laborers who were his followers.

His followers told many wonderful tales about the good deeds he performed, and before long the kindly Israel ben Eliezer was known as the Baal Shem Tov, the "Master of the Good Name," for it was said that he could heal people by merely pronouncing the Holy Name of God. He is also known as the Besht, an acronym made up of the first letters of *Baal Shem Tov*.

The followers of the Baal Shem Tov, who called themselves Hasidim ("pious ones"), would dance with joy in their synagogues when they welcomed the Sabbath. Even in the midst of prayers they would dance and sing wordless melodies in praise of God. The leaders of the Hasidim in the generations after the Baal Shem Tov were known as Tzaddikim ("righteous ones"), and their disciples followed them with great fervor.

Israel ben Eliezer died in 1760 at the age of sixty-two.

MATCH THE COLUMNS

1. Catherine the Great   One-room schoolhouse
2. Pogrom   Baal Shem Tov
3. Cheder   Russian empress
4. Eliezer ben Israel   Massacre of Jews
5. Baal Shem Tov   Master of the Good Name

FILL IN THE BLANKS

1. The partitions of Poland brought _____ the lion's share of _____ Jewry.

2. Jews were only allowed to live in the _____ .

3. The cheder was a _____ where Jewish children learned _____.

4. At first Israel earned his living as a _____

5. The Baal Shem Tov believed Jews could reach spiritual heights by _____.

Prayer, Russia, school, lime digger, Torah, Pale of Settlement, Polish

ANSWER THE QUESTIONS

1. Why did Catherine the Great restrict the residential rights of the Jews of Poland?
2. How did the restriction hurt the Jews of Russia?
3. How did the restriction help the Jewish community grow closer together?
4. What is worship of the heart?
5. Who were the Hasidim?
6. How did Israel's life in the mountains as a lime digger shape his ideas about prayer?
7. Why did the Besht's ideas of Judaism appeal to the Jews of Russia?

ISRAEL BEN ELIEZER AND YOU

The Besht and his wife Hannah spent many years in a village in the Carpathian Mountains. He loved to walk through the woods, listening to the singing of the birds and talking to the animals. The Baal Shem Tov was inspired by the beauty of nature.

Did you know that there is a special blessing when someone sees a great natural wonder?

The Besht is quoted as saying:

If the sight of a wonder of nature suddenly appears, then ask yourself: "Is not this beauty from a divine source?" Such a perception of beauty is an experience of the Eternal.

1. What do you consider a wonder of nature: a rainbow, a waterfall, the ocean, forests, a field of flowers? Can you think of other wonders?
2. Do you have any special feelings when you see such a wonder?
3. Is appreciating the wonder as special as experiencing it?
4. Can humans create a natural wonder?
5. What is happening to our natural wonders? Why are they disappearing?
6. How are humans destroying the beauties of nature?
7. What can be done to stop the destruction of rainforests, farmland, and the air we breathe?
8. Do you know of any organization that is trying to preserve the environment? Do you know of any Israeli organization that is trying to rebuild and reforest the land?
9. Do you know anything about the JNF (Keren Kayemet L'Yisrael)?
10. What can you do to help preserve the environment?

World History: 17th–18th century

IN THE FIFTEENTH AND SIXTEENTH CENTURY, the Jews succeeded in performing an important service in central Europe. In those centuries the rulers of Poland underestimated the value of their raw materials. Enterprising Jewish traders carried the raw materials, such as wood, and metals, to Germany and exchanged them for manufactured products.

Jews were also important in the cloth and wool trade. They had connections with Jewish wool and cloth manufacturers in England, France and Germany. Jews also took an active role in the manufacture of wine. They entered into this activity because it was forbidden to drink wine prepared by a non-Jew.

Jews conducted their business according to talmudic law and developed their own community organizations. Each town had its own organization called the Kahal. The Kahal collected their own taxes and dealt with civil matters in their own local courts. The Kahal also had its own president, its charity institutions, its synagogues, its own hospitals and whatever was needed for its survival.

By the 18th century, Jewish traders and manufacturers were restricted by the government and lost most of their markets. The restrictions were very beneficial for the Christian traders and manufacturers who now took over the markets developed by the Jews.

After the death of the Baal Shem Tov in 1760, Hasidism spread throughout Poland and Ukraine, and began to make inroads into Lithuania.There it met with opposition, because Polish Jewry and Lithuanian Jewry had quite different cultures and lifestyles. Because of their poverty, Polish Jews placed their faith in Kabbalah and believed in secret incantations, faith healing, and religious amulets. The Lithuanians, who were better educated, focused on the rigors of halachic study and formal worship.

Unlike Polish Jewry, Lithuanian Jewry maintained the tradition of talmudic scholarship. In the 18th century, Vilna, the capital of Lithuania, had a population of 5,000 Jews, yet it produced numerous sages with the highest level of scholarship. As a result, Vilna came to be called the Jerusalem of Lithuania.

Elijah, the Gaon of Vilna, was a product of this scholarly community. He emphasized the importance of scholarship, while the Baal Shem Tov stressed emotional mysticism. Both men, each in his own way, met the needs, hopes, and aspirations of their communities. Each raised the spiritual level of Jewish life in Eastern Europe.

The Gaon of Vilna: 1720–1797

THE RABBIS WHO FOUGHT AGAINST HASIDISM were called Mitnagdim ("opponents"). Their leader was the Gaon of Vilna, Elijah ben Solomon, the greatest of Vilna's many scholars—also known as the Vilna Gaon.

Even as a young man everyone recognized that Elijah was an ilui, a child prodigy. By the age of ten he had outgrown the knowledge of his teachers and began studying independently. By the time he was bar mitzvah, Elijah had already gone through all 24 volumes of the Talmud. In addition, without a teacher, he studied mathematics, astronomy, science, and anatomy.

Elijah never accepted an official position as a rabbi. He spent many hours in his study, quietly engaged in scholarly work and teaching a small circle of advanced scholars who wanted to acquire his approach to the Talmud. His method was one of precise detail. He would first read each passage thoroughly and then refer to its original sources in the Mishnah and in the Torah itself. This exacting method made for a much clearer understanding of the halachah.

Like the great scholars of earlier days, the Vilna Gaon mastered mathematics and astronomy in addition to the works of Jewish philosophy. He and his disciples encouraged the study of science as essential for a proper understanding of the Torah. This approach

was quite unusual, for in those days most yeshiva scholars confined themselves strictly to the Talmud and the commentaries of Rashi and the Tosafists.

The Vilna Gaon never held public office. Unofficially, however, he was the acknowledged spiritual leader of Lithuanian Jewry. Many people came to the kindly Rabbi Elijah with their personal problems. He always advised them and, when necessary, quietly arranged for financial assistance to help them out of their difficulties.

In the days of the Vilna Gaon the conflict between Hasidism and Mitnagdim became very bitter. One source of difficulty was the Hasidic claim that the Tzaddikim were intermediaries between the ordinary Hasidim and God. The Mitnagdim maintained that all human beings were personally responsible to God and therefore no intermediary was needed.

The Vilna Gaon took up the fight against Hasidism, going so far as to forbid his followers to intermarry with them. In time, this ban was lifted, as it became evident that the Hasidic approach fully followed the laws and commandments of the Torah.

Hasidim and Mitnagdim persisted in their different ways, as they do today, but each group learned to respect and appreciate the other's contribution to Judaism.

Until his death, when he was almost 80, the Gaon of Vilna spent his days in study and writing. Hard as it may be to believe, he wrote more than 80 books. Among them were commentaries on almost every important work of Jewish literature, including several on the Kabbalah.

MATCH THE COLUMNS

1. Vilna   Child prodigy
2. Mitnagdim   Elijah ben Solomon
3. Hasidim   Opponents
4. Ilui   Pious ones
5. Vilna Gaon   Jerusalem of Lithuania

FILL IN THE BLANKS

1. Lithuanian Jews focused on the rigors of _____ scholarship and formal worship.

2. _____ was the greatest among the many scholars in Vilna.

4. The _____ believed that each person is responsible to God and needs no intermediary.

5. _____ and Mitnagdim respect and appreciate each other's contribution to _____.

Judaism, talmudic, Elijah ben Solomon, Hasidim, Mitnagdim

ANSWER THE QUESTIONS

1. Why did the Polish Jews accept the Hasidic type of Judaism?
2. Why was Vilna called the Jerusalem of Lithuania?
3. What qualities made Solomon ben Israel an ideal Jewish leader?
4. Why did the Hasidim and the Mitnagdim dislike each other?
5. Do you know of any groups that have different ideas about how Judaism should be practiced?
6. How do they differ?

THE VILNA GAON AND YOU

Jews are known as Am ha-Sefer ("People of the Book"). The acceptance of the book—the Torah—at Mount Sinai marked the birth of the Jewish people. The life and destiny of the Jew are found in the Torah and in all the many other works based on it.

Throughout their history, Jews have always had a love affair with books. The Spanish poet Ibn Ezra describes a book as "a friend who will cause you no harm, and bring you only pleasure."

The Vilna Gaon said:

A Jewish scholar must learn all the seven branches of knowledge. A knowledge of all the sciences, algebra, geometry, astronomy, music, etc., is necessary to understand the Torah, for they are all included in it. If a person lacks general knowledge, he will lack a hundred times as much in the knowledge of the Torah, for Torah and science go together.

From this statement, we know that the Vilna Gaon believed in a complete Jewish and general education.

1. Can a scholar really understand the Bible without knowing math, astronomy, music, etc.?
2. What branch of science would you have to know to study the creation of sun, moon, and stars?
3. What branch of science would you have to know to understand the plagues in the story of Passover?
4. What is the Vilna Gaon telling you about your studies?
5. Do you think that knowing physics can make you a better doctor? How?
6. Do you think that knowing music or playing an instrument can make you a better rabbi or teacher?
7. Do you think that knowing computer science can make you a better businessperson?
8. Will you take the Gaon's advice? How?